CRAZY SHEPHERD ~ CRAZY SHEEP

It's that simple

A Story of Unexpected Hope

RONALD C. GELAUDE

Author of *The Religion of Jesus*

ISBN: 1493628887

ISBN-13: 9781493628889

Library of Congress Control Number: 2013920590
CreateSpace Independent Publishing Platform
North Charleston, South Carolina

DEDICATED TO:

Michael (Mike) Frank Gelaude, my younger brother and best friend, who died far too soon. Mike, I've kept my promise.

PREFACE

As I explained in my first book *The Religion of Jesus,* for a long time, I thought the message of Jesus was simply about life after death: what my post life would encompass after all was said and done. At least this was the message wafting around in my head. The instinctive and irresistible draw to an off-road life of adventure, thrill, and exploration, in my view, was not compatible with the life that Jesus offered. After all wasn't he and those who followed him concerned only with my ultimate destination? I supposed that was a good thing, if that's all there was to it. For a young boy, however, the life that Jesus offered seemed boring, mundane, and irrelevant. So as one might expect, my attention, energy, and focus were nowhere near what church folks had in mind. Some might even say that they were at odds.

Then one day, many years later, I was introduced to Tom. At first glance he was just another bored-out-of-his-mind pastor who was going through the motions. What I ultimately discovered, however, was that first impressions aren't always the most accurate impressions, especially if you've made up your mind beforehand. Benjamin Franklin once said, "If you wish information and improvement from the knowledge of others, and yet at the same time express yourself as firmly fixed in your present opinions, modest, sensible men, who do not love disputation, will probably leave you undisturbed in the possession of your error."[1]

On one occasion when Tom came over for a visit, he caught me off guard. He drove up in his Jeep, ragtop down, caked with off-road mud, and jumped out, dressed in his grubby T-shirt and ragged shorts. Then with grin that said *I just had a great time off-road,* we sat on my porch and talked about sports and guy stuff for more than two hours. Tom was very different than any Christ follower I had met, and over time we became good friends. Ever so slowly it was Tom who introduced me to the Jesus I had never met before, and before long

I began to see what life could be like when viewed through a fundamentally different lens. This was the lens of a humble Servant who was considered totally out of his mind, to the point of inviting an entrepreneurial fisherman to get out of a boat and walk on the water with him! True story. This Jesus was different.

In the years after meeting Tom, I began to sense the nudge from God to become a pastor, and this is where my off-road journey began. At the time, my wife and I were living rather comfortably, and besides my wife's serious health issues, my sales career was in full swing, and we wanted for nothing. Our new life with Jesus was growing, and life was good. Little did my wife and I know that God had in mind something crazy for our lives. Some fifteen years later, Tom and his family had moved to Florida to serve in another church when he was diagnosed with throat cancer. Two weeks before his passing, he and I had a lengthy phone conversation. He explained that when he first knocked on my door, he was extremely nervous and a bit hesitant, but somehow he knew that if the Jesus *he* knew captured *my* mind and heart, my influence in this world would be huge (his words, not mine). Tom never knew of the depth and nature of the formative impact he had on my life, my dreams, how I would ultimately handle tragedy, and where God would take my wife and me over the following thirty-some years. Tom, the off-road one, changed my life.

As it turns out, Tom was certainly right about the first part. Jesus has captured the fullness of my mind and the essence of my heart, but as it relates to the second part—the so-called huge influence—well this isn't really up to me, is it? If my crazy life as an off-road follower of Christ affects one life, that's huge. Maybe that one life will be yours, and maybe someday you'll write a book telling others about your crazy life, and you'll mention my name and how this book introduced you to the Jesus you'd never met before. Wouldn't that be cool?

I know it sounds crazy, but as you will discover, this is the way of crazy sheep.

Ron

CONTENTS

INTRODUCTION

It seems as if every neighborhood has a gang. In my Detroit neighborhood, it was the Patton Street Gang, and they were inseparable. They were a tight group and moved as one. Where one went, they all went. If you messed with one, you messed with them all. I'm not saying they were feared, but they were always up to something. One well-known incident took place at Snellbock's Drug Store. The heist, as it was called, took place in broad daylight, and the owner, Mr. Snellbock, was not happy. While the other gang members were quietly roaming the store, Charlie, the gang leader at the time, decided to help himself to a few items on the shelf. He simply placed them in his pocket and walked out the store. It was that easy. Mr. Snellbock, however, was much smarter than Charlie. He promptly ran out of the store and grabbed Charlie by the ear, and even though the rest of the gang claimed they knew nothing of Charlie's plan, they all got in big trouble. No one will ever know if they were telling the truth; it's the nature of gang life.

Their names were Charlie, Billy, Johnny, Frankie, and Ronnie, and we were in the third grade. Our parents didn't buy the excuse that it was all Charlie's fault. So my parents told me that I had to go back to Mr. Snellbock to apologize and pay for all five candy bars. I remember it as if it was yesterday. My parents also told me that I was no longer allowed to hang out with Charlie because of his influence on me. Charlie was the ringleader, and we were guilty by association.

It's the same with Jesus. Jesus was considered crazy by many of the religious leaders who gathered around him; he was regularly accused of being *stark raving mad*.[2] Furthermore, this very same Jesus once referred to himself as the Good Shepherd—not *a* good shepherd, but *the* good shepherd. This is no accident. The simple word *the* is important; it communicates uniqueness and originality. Jesus is not just one shepherd among many. He is *the* shepherd to whom there is no equal.

In the very same speech where he refers to himself as *the* Good Shepherd, Jesus also refers to his followers as sheep by stating the following:

> I am the Good Shepherd. I know my own sheep and my own sheep know me. In the same way, the Father knows me and I know the Father. I put the sheep before myself, sacrificing myself if necessary. You need to know that I have other sheep in addition to those in this pen. I need to gather and bring them, too. They'll also recognize my voice.[3]

So as you can see, Jesus metaphorically refers to not only himself as the Good Shepherd but also his followers as his *sheep*. So if the shepherd is considered stark raving mad, what does that say about the sheep that follow him? In my opinion, just like the members of the Patton Street Gang, the followers of the Good Shepherd are guilty by association. In other words, at times they too are crazy. By the way, it wasn't just the religious leaders who thought he was off his rocker; some in his own family thought the same. Just read the following:

> Then Jesus entered a house, and again a crowd gathered, so that he and his disciples were not even able to eat. When his family heard about this, they went to take charge of him, for they said, "He is out of his mind."[4]

Crazy Shepherd, crazy sheep; it's that simple. But here's the crazy twist: his crazy sheep hang on every word, every promise, every thought, every dream, and every command of the crazy and ever-present Good Shepherd. This is especially true of the extraordinary promise of not just a *new life*, but also a new *way of life*. The Crazy Shepherd puts it this way:

I am the Gate for the sheep. All those others are up to no good— sheep stealers, every one of them. But the sheep didn't listen to them. I am the Gate. Anyone who goes through me will be cared for—will freely go in and out, and find pasture. A thief is only there to steal and kill and destroy. I came so they (my sheep) can have real and eternal life, a better life than they ever dreamed of.[5]

A better life than you've ever dreamed of is an often-overlooked promise that was made by Christ himself, and as such, it is worth our earnest consideration. It is the primary reason for writing this book. At the age of thirty-five, this is what caught my attention, captured my imagination, and captivated my heart and soul. The life that Jesus offers in the here and now is an adventure beyond compare; a journey to places unknown; and an off-road expedition that stimulates the heart, mind, body, and soul. There is life worth living, but to get there, you have to be a little crazy.

I hope this book will stimulate your heart and mind, but at some point, one has to make a decision and move forward with what has been learned, discussed, and investigated. If you read *The Religion of Jesus,* you know that the Latin word for *religion* means the binding of belief and practice, and you can't really separate them. In other words, what good is it to think or profess faith in something if you're not willing to put that faith into practice? It can be said that to believe and to not practice is no belief at all; it is nothing more than empty thoughts that come and go with the wind of convenience. As I noted in my first book, you can often tell what a person truly believes by their actions over the course of time, but it is here that I must warn you. The life that Jesus invites us into is called crazy for a number of reasons. It's often countercultural, sometimes counterintuitive, and at times it's extremely challenging. In fact, at some point, you may choose to walk away, and if so, you wouldn't be the first to do so. To this option, which I don't recommend, the writer John offers us some insight: "On hearing it [the teaching of Jesus], many disciples said, 'This is a hard teaching. Who can accept it?'"[6] A bit later John goes on to explain that many of Jesus's early followers walked away and no longer followed him. Why? It's not easy being crazy. It's hard work, demanding, costly, and often misunderstood. More often than not, being a crazy sheep requires swimming against the current, and in doing so, some will think you are *actually* crazy. This is to be expected and met with an inviting, off-road, I'm-having-way-too-much-fun grin on our faces. This too is the way of crazy sheep, but more on this later.

In this book I share some personal thoughts and stories by inviting you into my journal, and for obvious reasons, I've omitted the names of those I hold so dear in my life. It's also important to note that my journal is simply an ongoing collection of thoughts in given moments of time, and because of this you could surmise that my marriage to Bonnie was not without its rough spots. To this I would simply add that we had our highs and lows just like everyone else. My ultimate hope, however, is that through this book you will see Jesus, the Good and yet Crazy Shepherd, in a new or refreshing light. My dream of dreams would most certainly come true if you begin to see yourself differently as well—as someone who can experience in full measure all that Jesus has to offer in this upside-down world. You'll know what I mean by this as you read further. So take your time, and I hope you enjoy my thoughts and scribbles. Some of the examples and stories offered throughout the following chapters are only that, small examples of what a larger topic may look like, or only one expression among many as to how a particular theological concept may work out in life. God, and all that he is, remains far more complex and expansive than we can see or experience on this planet called Earth, and if you stop and think about it, there is great comfort in this somewhat paradoxical mystery.

I don't know what happened to Charlie or any other members of the Patton Street Gang; my parents moved our family when I was in the fifth grade. But, while I didn't realize it at the time, being part of a gang taught me an invaluable lesson. You become the company you keep. Today, at the age of sixty-four, my new gang is nothing more and nothing less than an incredible, off-the-paved-road bunch of crazy sheep! After all, what else would you expect from followers of the Crazy Shepherd?

CHAPTER I CRAZY LOVE (PART I) | *Moving Beyond Self and into a Life of Selfless Love*

My friend and I met quite regularly and our discussions were both straightforward and thought provoking, often to the point where we had discovered the topic of our next lunch together. There is one meeting, however, that stands out in my mind. Albeit a side comment, something was said that took me back in time, back to a place where I grew up hearing the words over and over. As he sipped his iced tea, my friend, who has been a Christian for many years, blurted out, "I'm a worm, nothing more than a worthless depraved man in the hands of a merciful God. I just need to work harder at being a better person, reading the Bible more, praying more, going to church more, and serving more." Thinking that he was pulling my leg as usual, my response was, "Are you feeling wormy enough to buy lunch?" Well, he wasn't kidding, and our conversation slowly ended with my half-baked attempt to help him see his true identity as a follower of Christ. It didn't really help much; he was quite comfortable and rather convinced of his worminess, and his answer was to work harder.

If you've been around the Christian church scene for a while, you know how much has changed over the past few decades. As I see it, we've moved past the worthless worm part and into a more reasonable way of describing the fundamental nature of the Christian life. Jesus summed it up better than we could have ever imagined, and if you've spent any significant time in church lately, you've heard more than one message on Jesus's response to this question: *Which of the all the laws are the most important?* The religious leaders of Jesus's day had managed to expand the laws of the Old Testament to approximately 613 laws that, in their mind, covered all the bases. In doing so, they had hoped to ensure a right standing before God that would pay off on the day of his coming judgment. Originally it was a noble endeavor, but by the time Jesus arrived on the scene, it had become a measuring stick of sorts that determined one's worth and significance in the eyes of God. The ability or inability to follow the laws defined who was within and who was beyond the scope of God's unwavering love. One's external performance was what determined one's essential value. Jesus's response, however, was intriguing to say the least. He answered the aforementioned question by saying:

> The most important one," answered Jesus, "is this: 'Hear, O Israel: The Lord our God, the Lord is one. Love the Lord your God with all your heart and with all your soul and with all your mind and with all your strength. The second is this: 'Love your neighbor as yourself.' There is no commandment greater than these.[7]

During my twenty years of being a pastor, Jesus's answer to the lawyer's question has become the new mantra of church and its ministry to the community and the world. Jesus's statement has changed the way we share his Good News. It has reshaped how churches develop their philosophy of ministry and outreach. It has sparked new and simpler vision statements, such as *Love God, Love others, Serve the World*. Loving God and loving others is so much less complicated than strictly abiding by the 613 laws that seem far-reaching and burdensome. Love God with all of my being, and love others as myself. I can somehow wrap my head and heart around this; it's a good way of life. This was true when Jesus was arguing with the lawyer who asked the question, and it's true for all who follow him today. It was then and still is the primary message of Jesus[8]. What I want to explore is not the integrity or character of Jesus's words; they most certainly stand on their own and need little explanation. What makes me curious, however, is the character and nature of the ones who are told to love others as themselves. It's not the object of one's love that makes me curious but the character and nature of the one doing the loving. We will spend the rest of this chapter and the next looking into this, but before we move forward, it might be beneficial to take a moment and define the meaning of love, as this is especially important in the context of loving others as ourselves.

The Greek word for *love* has three basic definitions. It can mean *brotherly* love (phileo), and it can mean *erotic* love (eros). The nature of the love that Jesus speaks of in his answer to the expert in the law, however, means *sacrificial* love (agape).[9] This type of love, being both unconditional and sacrificial, was demonstrated in his willing sacrifice of himself. It is so much deeper and reaches so much further into the human experience than mere brotherly or erotic love. Throughout the remainder of this book, the nature of love that we will be exploring is both unconditional and sacrificial. On more than one occasion, the writer Paul says, "Love [agape] has its perfect expression among men in the Lord Jesus Christ."[10] In other words, in Christ we see how *(agape)* love plays out, in that it's not about the character and nature of the ones being loved that matters most. This is precisely why it can often be perceived as off-road crazy.

One of my passions is long-distance trail running, and it is during these times that I often enjoy the most clarity. There's something divine about running around like a loose cannon in the midst of creation—the deeper in the woods and forests, the better. No earphones, no cell phone, no interference, no noise; you get the picture. So the other day as I was running the Hartwick Pines State Park trails, it dawned on me: what if the ones doing the loving of others have no genuine love of themselves? In other words, is it possible to love others effectively the way Jesus asks us to love them if we don't first love who we are? Think about it for a moment.

This thought stopped me in my tracks, and my mind began racing back to the people I've met along the way who think that they are worms, that they are less-than, that they are worthless, that they are unlovable, ugly, fat, skinny, lacking any measurable talent, run-of-the-mill, uneducated, ill-equipped, invisible, or stupid. I've seen it in their eyes and in their demeanor. Because of their experiences, surroundings, and unfortunate circumstances, there are many people who simply don't love who they are. It's not uncommon to see yourself as *less than* when life throws you a curveball. How would you answer this question: Do you really love who you are? I suspect that your first thought might revolve around your view of humility. In other words, if you say *yes, I do love myself,* then maybe you're prideful. We've been taught that humility is thinking less of ourselves, and if you admit that you truly love who you are, it's tantamount to boasting. Is a humble person simply one who thinks less of himself? How would you describe a humble person? If you're one who carries around the baggage of shame, guilt, fractured emotions, painful memories of physical or verbal abuse, self-loathing, not looking handsome or pretty enough, a broken body, never measuring up to expectations, and the wounded spirit that can come with these, then you know precisely what I'm talking about. Your default is thinking less of yourself. But this is not necessarily humility; it's a portrait of a deep-seated wounded heart and soul, and as such, loving yourself can be a grand challenge.

In his book, *The Freedom of Self Forgetfulness,* pastor and author Tim Keller crystallizes the meaning of humility as not thinking more of ourselves or thinking less of ourselves, but instead thinking of ourselves less.[11] Think about this. Read it a few times before you move on, and let it sink in. Why is this so important? It is here that we can begin to put into practice the answer Jesus offered to the questioning lawyer. *And the second is this; love others as yourself.* What I hope you begin to see is that loving who you are is neither an act of pride nor is it an act of humility. It is, however, extremely helpful, if not necessary, if we want to live Jesus's answer to the question.

You Can Love Who You Are

For the longest time, my life was driven and shaped primarily by what I thought others thought of me. In others words, my actions and behaviors were based on how I thought it would be perceived by others; how it would elevate my value and worth in their eyes; how it would make me stand out in the crowd; and how it would help them see my talents, skills, and abilities. I didn't know it then, but I can see it now; this was my way of finding my place and identity, one that was seen through the eyes of others. In retrospect one of my biggest fears was being average or, worse yet, common.

I've never really excelled at anything. My grades in school, from elementary to high school, were at best less than average. When my fourth grade math teacher told me that I had flunked math, my heart sank. She said it was OK to fail, but to a ten-year-old boy, it was far from OK. Upon entering community college, I flunked out after the first semester and proceeded to get a factory job in the small town where I lived. Life was becoming routine.

It was 1968, and the Vietnam War was in full swing. Tired of being bored and common, I enlisted in the Air Force. It seemed the safest alternative to being drafted into the army (my lottery number was too low to take any chances). It was in the military, however, where I began to excel. My ability to quickly diagnose and resolve complex technical problems propelled me to becoming a Bombing Systems and Navigational specialist working on B-52s. It was thrilling work, and I served in Southeast Asia twice during the so-called conflict. My job was to fix the bombing or navigational computer system before we arrived over our target. It was here that I really learned to perform for others, and in doing so, I was now elevated to someone who mattered, someone who stood out among others, someone with privileges. In the eyes of others, I was no longer common. I had value.

This would be a reoccurring pattern that followed me for the next thirty years of computer sales and then vocational ministry. My identity, who I am, was determined by what others thought of me, and this shaped my view of myself (it's a vicious cycle). When my performance was solid, I thought more of myself, and when it was substandard, I thought less of myself. When life was good and the awards were coming in, I was warned not to become prideful. And when success was fleeting, I was told it was rather humbling. Unknowingly this ongoing cycle began to shape my view of pride and humility. I thought humility was thinking less of myself, and pride was just the opposite. Loving who I am is a roller coaster ride, and there are days that I still have to fight through this thinking. Can you relate?

Jesus, however, looks at life through a different lens, and this is especially true of who we are, our identity. He looks at us from the inside out, whereas we tend to look at ourselves from the outside in. In other words, our visible sides of life, our performance, our looks, our intellect, our faults, our demeanor, our success, our failures, our stature, and our abilities dramatically influence our not-so-visible inside. The very core of who we are is often shaped by what comes in, as opposed to letting our true identity (how Jesus views us) shape everything that flows out from there. Jesus longs for our identity in him to work its way out, and as such, shape all that we do for ourselves as well as others, and this most assuredly includes loving.

Have you ever heard the saying that Jesus loves the hard-to-love? I hear it with some regularity. The implication is that since Jesus loved the hard-to-love, we should as well. Seems simple enough. But if you're like me, this is extremely difficult. It's hard to love the hard-to-love. During another one of my trail-running episodes, however, it dawned on me; Jesus never found it hard to love anyone, ever. His love for every living human being was rich in every way that rich can be defined. In other words, his sacrificial love was without conditions. It wasn't based on the character and nature of the one being loved. It was based on the one doing the loving: himself. His love lacked nothing and was totally complete even to the point of his death on the cross. He was perfectly in tune with his identity, and his love flowed out from there in true humility. Again I want you to pause and think this through. If you find this hard to believe, read the following words of John, one of Christ's closest followers:

> Before the Passover celebration, Jesus knew that his hour had come to leave this world and return to his Father. He had loved his disciples during his ministry on earth, and now he loved them to the very end. It was time for supper, and the devil had already prompted Judas, son of Simon Iscariot, to betray Jesus. Jesus knew that the Father had given him authority over everything and that he had come from God and would return to God. So he got up from the table, took off his robe, wrapped a towel around his waist, and poured water into a basin. Then he began to wash the disciples' feet, drying them with the towel he had around him.[12]

In these few simple verses, we see that Jesus knew exactly who he was, but chose to serve his followers with complete humility, loving them perfectly, even the one who would soon betray him. It wasn't hard for him to love, nor was he thinking less of himself. He was simply thinking of himself less. This cosmic shift is what makes all the difference in the way we too can effectively love others *as ourselves*. Before we get to the idea of loving the hard-to-love, however, there is one question in my mind that stands out: Can we actually love others as ourselves if we don't know who we are in the eyes of the Crazy Shepherd?

Knowing Your True Identity

As I was driving home from lunch with my wormy friend, I remembered that there is a vast difference between being worthless and unworthy. *Worthless* describes how someone perceives her or his value, and *unworthy* describes someone who sees him or herself as not deserving or not meriting something. For example if someone was to knock on your door and announce that someone had just purchased you a new suit or dress, you might respond by asking, "What did I do to deserve such a gift?" A sense of not being worthy is based on merit. On the other hand, you may proclaim that you will not accept the gift because you are a worthless person. After all, why wear a new suit or dress? It wouldn't make any difference. I'm not even worth the time and energy that it would take to bring me the gift to begin with. A sense of worthlessness is based on your perceived identity, that you have no redeeming value. One is performance driven. The other is identity driven. It is in the cavern of this difference that God has something to say.

One day the religious leaders and legal experts wanted to trap Jesus. They wanted to accuse him of disregarding the Law, and in doing so they would discredit him in the eyes of everyone. As Jesus was teaching in the temple court, they brought before him a woman who was caught in the very act of adultery. No doubt she was guilty of breaking one of the 613 Laws. To this there was no argument. Can you imagine what was going on in her mind? There she stood before Jesus and the large temple crowd, only moments before, in bed with a man not her husband, and now most likely exposed in the midst of her disgrace and shame. What a sight. The religious leaders couldn't have cared less about this woman; to them she was nothing more than a worthless nobody. They thought that they had crafted a situation whereby Jesus would find himself on the horns of a dilemma, and they thought there was no way out. Either he follows the letter of the law and stones her, which would tarnish his reputation of being compassionate, or he disobeys the Law by not stoning her and becomes liable to religious ridicule and condemnation[13].

The Crazy Shepherd, however, refuses to become trapped and places the dilemma back on the shoulders of those trying to trap him. Two things take place, both of which are so very rich. First he looks directly at the crowd and says, "Go ahead and stone her, but only if you are someone who is without sin." To this stone-throwing qualification, the crowd slowly backs away and begins to disperse, for no one can make such a claim. Then he turns to the woman and asks if anyone condemns her. "No," she replies. Then he responds, "Neither do I," and tells her to leave her life of sin.[14] As it turns out, those who were far from qualified to condemn her but wanted to couldn't. But the only one who was qualified didn't. The Crazy Shepherd was the only one who truly cared about her, and I wonder how she felt deep inside as she was hearing his words? Shame breeds a deep-seated sense of worthlessness and often scars our identity, but the Crazy Shepherd longs to recapture not only who we are in his eyes but also in the eyes of his Father. So who are you in the eyes of the Crazy Shepherd? Just like it was with the woman standing by his side, you are a priceless somebody of immeasurable worth. Unworthy? We all are. Worthless? Not a chance! And it is here that we can learn to become comfortable in our own skin.

Being a church planter comes with certain expectations, and as I mentioned earlier, I've never truly excelled at anything. By some standards church planters are expected to be outgoing, energetic, pure visionaries—type A extroverts who push hard and have an innate ability to attract hundreds of people into their dream. Over the years I've tried very hard to be this person, but fell short on most of these measurements. With the help of a great coach, however, I've learned how to become very comfortable with myself. I'm an introvert, fairly quiet, somewhat outgoing, vision capable, easy going, and not all that demanding. I'm a trail-running teacher of God's Word who longs to see people enter into a crazy life with the Crazy Shepherd. With this renewed sense of freedom, I'm now comfortable in my skin. I know how it feels to be otherwise, and as you will see, this can make all the difference.

The Two-Letter Roadblock

Every word in the Bible means something, even the profoundly small ones. For example, one vast difference between how Jehovah's Witnesses and Christians view Jesus hangs on a one-letter word: *a*. It's found in the book of John, in the very first verse. The variant readings are as follows:

9

In the beginning was the word and the word was God. (John 1:1 NIV)

In the beginning was the word and the word was a God. (John 1:1 New World Translation of the Holy Scriptures [Jehovah's Witnesses' Bible version])

As you can see, the only difference between the two verses found in the different versions is the letter *a*, and what a difference it makes. This is one reason why Jehovah's Witnesses don't believe that Jesus is God who became a man and lived among us, preexisted the created world, and had a part in creating it. The reasons behind this variant reading, however, are not why I share this verse, but it does illustrate how very small words have an affect on faith and religion. The point I'm trying to make is this: words, even the small ones, mean something, and it's the same with the answer that Jesus offered to the young legal expert who asked the question. Read it again:

And the second is this; love your neighbor as yourself.

The small word that makes a nuanced difference in Jesus's answer is *as*, and it deserves a bit of attention. Without going into great detail, the Greek word for *as* means different things depending on the context in which it is used. It can be a word of time (e.g., *as* the sun comes up, work the fields); it can be a word of cause (e.g., don't start fights *as* your brother picks on you); it can be a word of limitation (e.g., don't complain *as* one who has lost everything). In the case of Jesus's answer, however, the word *as* is a word describing likeness (e.g., love your mom *as* she loves you).[15] You could effectively replace the word *as* with the phrase *in the same way*, and in doing so, the reading would be as follows: And the second is this; love your neighbor "as" yourself, or "in the same way" you love yourself.

As someone who lives in an extrovert world this helped me realize that I actually know how to love introverts like me; those who may wrestle with how others define their success. I can love them *in the same way* I needed to be loved because I am one, and maybe they too can experience the genuine freedom I now have. The point of it all is that when we love others *as* ourselves, we're simply loving them in the same way we would love to be loved, and in doing so, we will love others with a high degree of integrity (i.e., a soundness of character or structure). Remember that it's not the character and nature of the ones being loved but of the ones doing the loving. It's easier to truly love others this way because we know what it looks like and how it should feel, and there is a profound richness in this kind of love. It's a love like no other. It is the birthplace of empathy, and it is here that all roadblocks are subsequently removed.

The love of my life is Bonnie, and we were married for thirty-seven years. Thirty-six of those years she suffered from systemic lupus, undergoing five hip surgeries, a twisted and often blocked esophagus, two surgeries to remove masses in her abdomen, the ugly side effects of steroids, deformed hands and feet, dozens of trips to the hospital, the inability to have children, two adoption denials, severe blood clots in her legs, Coumadin failure, and the need to self-inject drugs to keep herself alive. In the midst of all of this, Bonnie supported me in more ways than most will never know. Her life's mission, even in the depth of her illness, was to protect me and minimize her own problems so that I could do what God had called us to do: pastor a church, teach God's Word, and serve the poor with compassion around the globe. She did this often at great personal cost. She unexpectedly passed on July 7, 2011, of complications from lupus.

Being a pastor's wife is not always a picnic, and it's not easy finding a friend who will stick by your side and love you for the long haul, through the thick and thin of ministry life. It's a sad but true commentary, but people (including pastors) leave churches for a variety of reasons some without so much as a goodbye. What they often don't realize, however, is how it deeply hurts those who trusted you. We were both well aware of this dynamic, but this is why Bonnie was cautious in making friends. That is, until she met Martha.

Martha loved Bonnie *as* she herself would want to be loved. When she was with Bonnie, she thought about herself less, and everything changed. Bonnie had a listening friend, someone with whom she could finally share her frustrations, fears, and dreams without recourse. Martha deeply cared about her. If needed, she would run errands for her, clean house for her, do laundry for her, prepare meals for her, go to the doctor with her, or whatever was needed. What's even more interesting, however, is that Martha says the same thing about Bonnie, for Martha too had a caring friend, one with whom she could also share her frustrations and dreams. Bonnie too loved Martha *as* she herself loved to be loved. Both knew precisely what it looked like.

This is one example of what it can look like when knowing and loving *who you are* in Christ shapes the rest of you (from the inside out) and thus influences how you love others. Bonnie was, and Martha is, well aware of who they are in Christ, and it propelled both of them to live the command of Jesus to love your neighbor *as* [in the same way you love] yourself.

Do you think you could ever get there?

Enter the Crazy Shepherd

There are many Bible verses that clearly explain our identity as Christ followers, but there is one that stands out to me:

> He (Jesus) came into the very world he created, but the world didn't recognize him. He came to his own people, and even they rejected him. But to all who believed him and accepted him, he gave the right to become children of God.[16]

In these three short verses, John explains that all who receive him (i.e., look to Jesus in faith, which also means *trust*) have been given an inalienable and irrefutable right: the right to become a child of God. The word *become* is one of transition, in that those who believe, or place their trust in Christ, are morphed into the most intimate of all relationships—one between them and the living God who created them. It's a mystery of sorts, but in the depth of this relationship rests a pure identity that can never be stolen by others or by one's circumstance; it rests secure regardless of what life throws at you. I think you would agree that over the course of our lives, there is much that gets in the way, some of which can push our true identity into the closet of our mind. It gets buried underneath the hardness and disappointments of life on this earth. But it is here that the apostle Paul also reminds us of who we are, and how we can rise above all else and reclaim our identity as a priceless child of the living God, someone who takes his breath away whenever he looks at us. God loved us to the point of where he spared nothing to rescue us from anything that life throws our way. Paul puts it this way:

> Can anything ever separate us from Christ's love? Does it mean he no longer loves us if we have trouble or calamity, or are persecuted, or hungry, or destitute, or in danger, or threatened with death?...And I am convinced that nothing can ever separate us from God's love. Neither death nor life, neither angels nor demons, neither our fears for today nor our worries about tomorrow—not even the powers of hell can separate us from God's love. No power in the sky above or in the earth below—indeed, nothing in all creation will ever be able to separate us from the love of God that is revealed in Christ Jesus our Lord.[17]

Crazy love, a love not based on the character and nature of the one being loved but simply on the one doing the loving, is the art of *moving beyond self and into a life of selfless love*. But here's what's so very odd to those who don't quite understand the way of crazy sheep: it is here that loving the hard-to-love becomes possible, even to the point loving one's enemies. Sounds crazy, doesn't it?

CHAPTER 2 CRAZY LOVE (PART 2) | *Moving Beyond the Easy-to-Love*

Jesus was famous for taking things to the extreme, and along the way, he managed to irritate most everyone. Just about the time people thought they had figured him out, he would take it a step further only to have many walk away shaking their heads baffled, amazed, and often quite angry. For example one day when asked by the religious leaders whether they should pay taxes to Rome, Jesus responded by saying *give back to Caesar what is Caesar's and (give back) to God what is God's.*[18] It was an answer that pushed both the religious leaders and Roman officials over the cliff. To the religious leaders who were expected to not worship a self-proclaimed god like Caesar, giving money to him would have been theologically offensive, if not criminal. Furthermore, by separating giving taxes to Caesar and tithing to God, Jesus had managed also to separate Caesar from his self-assigned position of divinity, which would have been a capital offense. He raised the bar, and in doing so, he shocked and aggravated both sides. It would be no different when he taught about the necessity of loving one's enemies. Matthew describes this monumental episode as follows:

[Jesus continued teaching] "You have heard the law that says, 'Love your neighbor' and hate your enemy. But I say, love your enemies! Pray for those who persecute you! In that way, you will be acting as true children of your Father in heaven. For he gives his sunlight to both the evil and the good, and he sends rain on the just and the unjust alike. If you love only those who love you, what reward is there for that? Even corrupt tax collectors do that much. If you are kind only to your friends, how are you different from anyone else? Even pagans do that."[19]

So, as you can see, it's not enough to simply love the easy-to-love. Anyone can do this because loving him or her doesn't really cost anything; it's painless. The Crazy Shepherd, however, asks his crazy sheep to take it much deeper by inviting them to love those who are very hard to love, and quite honestly, this seems like a far-reaching, ridiculous suggestion. How can someone actually love an enemy? How can someone love and then forgive someone who has done them great harm? It doesn't seem possible, and sometimes is just doesn't seem fair. However, as it is with much of the crazy life, both are necessary if we are to walk in the crazy footsteps of the Crazy Shepherd. To be sure, love and forgiveness work hand in glove. But it begs the question, how much forgiveness is enough?

Just as soon as Jesus finished explaining how his followers should treat each other, Peter, the outspoken one, asked him a question. At first glance the question seems practical, as if Peter was genuinely seeking some reasonable boundaries to what he had just heard. Peter asks, "Lord, how often should I forgive someone who sins against me?"[20] But Peter's question was far from an honest inquiry. In rabbinic tradition in the first century, the consensus was that a brother could be forgiven of a repeated sin three times, but then on the fourth, no forgiveness was compulsory. Then, in an answer to his own timely question, Peter proposes a rather big-hearted and self-congratulatory answer by asking, "[Shall I forgive him up to] seven times?" In typical Jesus fashion, however, he counters Peter's offer with one of his own: *forgive not seven times, but seventy times seven*, and then follows it up with a story of a king who will forgive all of them far more than they will ever forgive.[21] In other words, forgiveness, be it of a friend or an enemy, has neither parameters in its subject nor limits in its frequency. The parable then told by Jesus was a glimpse into the very heart of God himself and a sneak peak into the life of the Crazy Shepherd. For not long after this interaction with Peter, he would forgive those who crowned him with thorns, beat him with whips, repeatedly punched his face, mocked his kingship, pierced his side, and ridiculed him as he hung on the cross between two thieves. Jesus knew precisely what forgiveness meant and why it is essential for those who would some day follow him. After all, he never asked anyone to do something that he himself wasn't willing to do. I wonder what was running through Peter's mind after this extraordinary exchange? Maybe he was looking for an out that didn't materialize. For who in their right mind could envision such a thing, and maybe, just maybe, we're more like Peter than we care to admit, in that we will only take the crazy love/forgiveness idea so far.

Why is forgiving our enemies and loving the hard-to-love so important? Why is this conversation so crucial, not just for crazy sheep, but also for anyone who may be reading this book? The chains of an unforgiving heart and the weight of an embittered soul keep us exactly where we are, alone in the midst of our deepest pain, hurt, frustration, and disappointment. It can be an invisible prison that prevents us from flourishing and experiencing all that life has to offer. On the other hand, when working side-by-side, love and forgiveness can become the purest path to a life of unprecedented freedom and magnificent release. Imagine a life without the baggage of an unforgiving heart and heaviness of a fractured resentful soul. If you don't think this is possible, then let me introduce you to Karen.

It was summer in Michigan, but it was winter in South Africa. During the eighteen-hour flight, there was ample opportunity to plan my activities because there would most assuredly be some free time between our short-term mission projects in the nearby villages. As a trail runner, how much more thrilling could it be to run trails in an environment where you might be dinner! Once we arrived at our camp, however, I realized that it wouldn't be dangerous, but nonetheless, I would be running the trails with zebra, wildebeests, kudu, gazelle, and many other remarkable animals; it was going to be a great trip. Long before we arrived in South Africa, our team met every other week to plan the various projects and get better acquainted. I was invited to come along as someone who would be there if anyone needed to chat about their experiences and the possible challenges therein, but I also worked in the villages with the rest of the team every day. But this story is not about the mission work; it is about the rather unexpected partner on my trail runs.

On the day before my first morning run, Karen, one of the ladies on our team, asked if she could run with me. I agreed. While in South Africa, we would run together often, and as the days unfolded, she slowly began sharing her heartbreaking story of a long history of sexual abuse by her father. He was a serial pedophile. She did most of the talking, and I would simply listen as her story unfolded. She asked about anger, guilt, shame, and why no one came to her assistance. She would ask about forgiveness, her struggle with severe pain, her profoundly deep-seated wounds, and why someone would do such a thing. I had no answers. We just talked as we ran.

Upon our return back home, and over the course of the ensuing months, I would witness a young twenty-something abused little girl somehow come to a place where she mustered up the courage to actually forgive her father. She called the prison in which he was paying for his crime, and while on the phone, she forgave him without malice or anger. It was a tenderhearted act of Christ like forgiveness, and what Karen would tell you is that while she had no plans of ever seeing him again, it is very much possible to forgive enemies who have done you great harm. What Karen came to realize is that forgiveness and reconciliation are separate issues. Love and forgiveness are gifts offered by the offended party, an act of pure grace and compassion. Reconciliation, however, is up to the one who has been offered the gift. Reconciliation is possible only when the offender embraces the gift of love and forgiveness, with a humble, repentant, remorseful, and contrite heart. Without it, reconciliation is not possible, nor is it expected. Crazy sheep like Karen are asked to simply offer the very same gift of love and forgiveness that they themselves have been offered by the Crazy Shepherd; how it may or may not be received is not up to them.

Crazy sheep are called by the Crazy Good Shepherd to walk in his footsteps because in doing so there is tremendous freedom.

While Karen's healing will continue, on that day she forgave, she was released from her paralyzing fear and the heavy baggage of her acute shame. Today, some nine years later, Karen is happily married and doing quite well. But this is not the end of the story. As this chapter was being written, she informed me that her dad was dying of cancer, and we talked further about how we need to continually place our guilt and fears on the shoulders of the Crazy Shepherd. Eventually she again called her dad and informed him that she prays for him. She told him that she prays that Jesus will be by his side when he meets God. He died three days later. Karen, my unexpected running friend, knows about forgiving the hard-to-forgive. She is, without question, one of those crazy sheep who walks in the footsteps of the Crazy Shepherd, and there are times when we too find it necessary to love completely without complete understanding. This is what forgiving our enemies and loving the hard-to-love can do to one's heart, soul, and life. It ushers in a level of unadulterated freedom like no other.[22]

A story like Karen's is incredibly moving, but it is far from unique. We hear about them and read about them quite regularly, and yet many of us remain where we are, carrying the baggage of unforgiveness, shame, and guilt on our own shoulders wherever we go. What we can learn from Karen and many like her, however, is that Jesus wants to carry our baggage for us. All we need to do is give it to him, even if it is only one piece of baggage at a time. As we give each one to him, we embark on a path of learning how to first love and forgive ourselves, and then we can begin to love and forgive others, even those who in our minds don't deserve it. Loving and forgiving our enemies is an essential component of the mosaic that describes the life of a person who is willing to open himself or herself up to the work of the Crazy Shepherd. Not just the work that takes place in the world around us but also, and more importantly, the difficult work that takes place inside of us. More than anything else, this Jesus is concerned about the heart, the very center of our being, and the very core of who we are and why we are here.

Are you holding a deep-seated grudge? Is there someone who has done you great harm that you need forgive? If so, first talk with a trusted friend, maybe a pastor or a counselor, and then write the one in question a note or give them a call. I know this can be extremely difficult, but it's not really about them; it's about the character and nature of who you are deep inside—the one doing the loving and forgiving. This is precisely where the crazy life begins.

(Journal Entry, Dec. 8, 2012)

Dear Jesus, yesterday marked month seventeen of my new life [since Bonnie's death], and it started out as a really dark day; my grief was overwhelming to say the least. In the midst of the looming shadows of Christmas, however, I hear the familiar sound of my phone signaling a text message. It simply reads, *How's your day starting, I'm concerned.* It was that simple and that brief, but it began to open a Pandora's box of sorts and it flooded my mind with thoughts of those who have cared for me over the years of life; the hundreds of meetings and conversations with those who You have placed in my life began to reappear as if each interaction took place by your divine decree. These memories open my eyes.

The rest of my day was filled with appointments; opportunities to sit and chat with people over lunch or a cup of coffee. Between these conversations, I get a call from a friend asking for help serving meals on Christmas Day. Each ensuing conversation begins to open the eyes of my heart as to how life seems to unfold. I begin to see that everyone we meet in some way, whether we realize it or not, influences our lives. When it looks like I'm giving, I'm actually receiving, even when talking with some-one who has in the past stepped on my heart, those I desperately need to love and forgive. It's a divine mystery. So, dear Jesus, help me pay close attention because it seems as if no interaction, conversation or otherwise, even when it comes in the shape of a six-word text, is insignificant or meaningless. They all add up and over time and will somehow shape the sum of who we are in life. When our lives, and the lives of those around us, begin to reflect the very nature of your love and glory, a contagion of hope in this otherwise dark world arrives on the scene; it's like a virus of cascading grace, love, and forgiveness that began when you entered the world on Christmas Day. Then I recall that it's not the character and nature of the ones being loved that matters; it's the character and nature of the ones expressing your crazy divine love to others that really counts.

The truth is that we are in good company, for this was the very life of Christ himself, the Good Shepherd, the one who was considered crazy by those who longed to steal his identity. This is where it all starts for his sheep, walking in the footsteps of Jesus with the same attitude, the same heart and soul, and the same selfless approach in every arena of life. Knowing we're perfectly loved, loving who we are, and then loving others, including the hard-to-love, in the same way we want to be loved is where God starts to do wonders in a life. You can recognize this person in an instant; they are more interested in you than anyone in the room. They listen intently amid the noise of the crowd. When they are with you, along every step of the way, you know that you are loved. And when they leave the room, you realize that they know more about you than you do of them; it's what they do and who they are deep inside. It's crazy beautiful, isn't it?

We had to spend some time here and for a very good reason. It's OK, if not essential, to love who you are and know why you are here. It's truly the beginning of a life well lived, and moreover, a life worth pursuing with every ounce of energy you can muster. The remaining chapters explore the nature of why we are here and peek further behind the curtain of who we are. After all, we are all *somebodies,* handcrafted by the living God in the very image of the Crazy Shepherd. When he looks into your eyes, you take his breath away, and then turning to the heavens, he confidently proclaims, "See, everyone, I told you so, no worminess here. What's not to forgive? What's not to love?"

Crazy love, in all of its expressions, it is the way of crazy sheep.

CHAPTER 3   CRAZY HOPE | *Moving Beyond the One-sided Coin*

There is nothing better than a great movie and a bag of popcorn. While the popcorn certainly tastes good to most everyone, what makes a movie great rests solely in the eyes of the viewer. My favorite movies are westerns, and among the greatest western ever made is *Tombstone* starring Kurt Russell as Wyatt Earp and Val Kilmer as Doc Holiday. It's another contemporary rendition of the legendary Wyatt Earp and how he and his brothers, along with his best friend Doc Holiday, find themselves at the infamous OK Coral. It's a story of the Old West, good guys versus bad guys, justice played out in the streets, and how things got done back in the day. I love it!

Yes, it's a movie about all those things, but moreover, it's a story of a friendship between two unlikely individuals, Wyatt and Doc. No one really likes Doc, and who can blame them? He's portrayed as a drunk, a gambler, and a womanizer who is dying of tuberculosis. He's angry, obnoxious, abusive, and everything that pushes others to hate him. I guess he was someone who was hard to love. One of, if not *the* best line in the movie, however, comes toward the end. After Wyatt, Doc, and friends had all but eliminated the gang known as the Cowboys, Doc agrees to let Wyatt take him to a sanatorium for treatment of his disease. Maybe you missed it, but it is here where you discover that the movie is about friendship. With tears running down his cheek, the final words of Doc to Wyatt reveal the underlying story. Doc says, "Wyatt, you're the only human being who ever gave me hope." How telling.

Hope is a word that is thrown around at every opportunity. It's often used with reckless abandon among politicians and leaders who offer hope to all who would simply listen and follow, only to find that whoever offered it is here today but gone tomorrow. By the way, this phenomenon is far from new. In Benjamin Franklin's autobiography, he tells of a governor who promises him some financial backing to start a printing company in Philadelphia. He was a young entrepreneur just getting started, and all he had to do was take a series of important documents to England. So Benjamin Franklin left for England with great hope, but upon his arrival, he found out that the governor often made promises he never kept—go figure. Franklin's hope for financial backing evaporated as quickly as it was offered, and as such, he was forced to remain in England until he could work his way back to the colonies, which took several months.[23]

With regularity hope is promised to us in the form of more money, more things, more fame, more security, more power, more privilege, more influence, and of course all that comes with those things, which supposedly is a more successful and comfortable life. Young athletes are systematically offered the hope of a professional sports career, and rising artists are lured into a hopeful promise of fame and fortune. Sadly only very few realize these hopes and dreams. Hope, it turns out, can be very elusive and often rather fleeting. It is here that I'm reminded of the timeless words of Solomon: *Hope deferred makes the heart sick, but a longing fulfilled is a tree of life.*[24]

The Tree of Life

Each and every Sunday, churches across our great country are filled with millions of people, people who come to worship and receive encouragement so they can take on the week at hand. They come, they go, and repeat the cycle each week. Early in my days of following Christ, I vividly remember the focus of most every Sunday message. It's stuck in my brain. The main thrust of Sunday services was that life in the here and now is all about our *hope in heaven*. If I heard that phrase once, I've heard it a thousand times, *hope in heaven*.

As I see it now, some twenty years later, however, if my only hope is hope in a future heaven, as crucial as this may be, then this is actually a hope deferred, and as Solomon says, this makes my heart sick at its very core. Fortunately, however, Solomon also says that a longing (a hope) fulfilled is the *tree of life*. It can be confusing. Is hope found in the here and now or in the future of one's eternity, or could it possibly be both?

When Solomon mentions the idea that a longing fulfilled is a *tree of life*, he was speaking of a tangible hope that can be realized in the here and now, and this idea was not lost among the Jewish readers of Solomon's era. To them a grand picture was painted; the *tree of life* was a poetic simile that represented the source of great blessing, a moral and spiritual source of a full life. This fullness of life is attributed to a certain possession or quality of mind and heart, and this brings the whole person into a right relationship with the Author and source of all life, God himself.[25] The *tree of life* then is a hope to be enjoyed for eternity, to be sure, but it's also a tangible hope for the fullness of life right here and right now. We must not miss this.

Hope is not merely wishful thinking of *hope in heaven*, nor is it an empty promise of a temporary hope for today. It is a tangible and viable *way of life* as it unfolds both today *and* for eternity. So it appears as if hope has two vital components, but for whatever reason, it seems as if a wall has been constructed between our lives in the present and our lives in eternity. Maybe I'm missing something, but as I see it, the coin of hope has two sides, and they are inseparable, one and the same. It is a both/and proposition and a both/and way of life, a life of unadulterated hope found only in the person of the Crazy Shepherd. So the question is how does Christ bring together a hope deferred and a hope fulfilled?

Jesus begins to answer the question when he says, "Do not let your hearts be troubled. You believe in God; believe also in me. My Father's house has many rooms; if that were not so, I would have told you. I am going there to prepare a place for you. And if I go and prepare a place for you, I will come back and take you to be with me that you also may be where I am."[26] These verses most assuredly describes our promised hope in the hereafter, but on another occasion, Jesus also expressed hope in all its fullness for the present when he says, "The thief comes only in order to steal, kill, and destroy. I have come in order that you (my sheep) might have life—life in all its fullness [now]."[27]

There is a certainty in the hope offered in the one and only Christ; it is an offer of unparalleled hope for both the here and now as well as in the hereafter. Jesus does not separate the present and the future in his offer of divine hope. It's one coin with two sides, and they are inseparable. When Jesus offered one, he offered the other. This is the good news for all who follow him. However what does any of this have to do with becoming a crazy sheep? Everything. Any hope that they may be offered in the here and now should also include an expression, or an offer, of eternal hope through the One who authored hope way back when, and herein is where it can get challenging at times.

Jesus and a Cup of Cold Water

When you examine the life of the Crazy Shepherd, it doesn't take long to discover that he began his message of tangible hope by addressing both physical and felt needs. You need look no further than the story of when he touched the leper who begged Jesus to make him clean.

So he [Jesus] traveled throughout the region of Galilee, preaching in the synagogues and casting out demons. A man with leprosy came and knelt in front of Jesus, begging to be healed. "If you are willing, you can heal me and make me clean," he said. Moved with compassion, Jesus reached out and touched him. "I am willing," he said. "Be healed!" Instantly the leprosy disappeared, and the man was healed.[28]

What is striking in this story is the two-fold nature of the leper's request. He asked Jesus for two things to happen, 1) to be *healed*, and 2) to be made *clean*. In the eyes of the leper, these were two very different requests, in that being healed addressed a physical need, and being cleansed addressed an emotional need. In the first century, anyone who had leprosy was considered filthy, sinful, disgusting, untouchable, and unholy. They were less-than-human trash with no intrinsic value. Many infants who were born with diseases or disabilities were literally thrown in the city dump to die of exposure. Those who were by chance lepers were nothing more than worms stuck in their worminess. Can you place yourself in the sandals of the leper? Can you imagine what this might feel like? Can you imagine what life must have been like never being touched by a human hand, never being invited over for dinner, never being looked at with dignity or respect, never being allowed to associate with the "clean" people? This man's physical disease affected the sum of his social worth, and like a sword, it pierced the depth of his heart and soul, the very foundation of his emotions and life. So Jesus, filled with compassion, actually did something that was unheard of and unimaginable by both the religious leaders as well as the disciples who followed him. He literally touched the man, and in doing so, the leper was both healed and cleansed. He was made whole again not only to himself but also to those around him. Can you imagine the pure joy in this man's face? How he must have felt when Jesus touched him in a way that he had never been touched before. Jesus *never* saw this man as unclean. He simply saw him as one who needed to be touched in his heart and soul. By addressing both his physical and emotional needs, Jesus offered this man a tangible hope for the here and now.

On another occasion, shortly after his not-so-polite condemnation of the hypocrisy of the religious leaders, Jesus again mapped out what hope looks like, and he left no room for fuzzy interpretation. In his explanation of what his Kingdom is like, he refers to a time when all will be judged after all is said and done.

When the Son of Man comes in his glory, and all the angels with him, he will sit on his glorious throne. All the nations will be gathered before him, and he will separate the people one from another as a shepherd separates the sheep from the goats. He will put the sheep on his right and the goats on his left. Then the King will say to those on his right, "Come, you who are blessed by my Father; take your inheritance, the kingdom prepared for you since the creation of the world. For I was hungry and you gave me something to eat, I was thirsty and you gave me something to drink, I was a stranger and you invited me in, I needed clothes and you clothed me, I was sick and you looked after me, I was in prison and you came to visit me." Then the righteous will answer him, "Lord, when did we see you hungry and feed you, or thirsty and give you something to drink? When did we see you a stranger and invite you in, or needing clothes and clothe you? When did we see you sick or in prison and go to visit you?" The King will reply, "Truly I tell you, whatever you did for one of the least of these brothers and sisters of mine, you did for me."[29]

Keep in mind this was not a new idea to the religious leaders of the day. A thousand years or so earlier, King Solomon spoke of it when he wrote, "Speak up for those who cannot speak for themselves, for the rights of all who are destitute. Speak up and judge fairly; defend the rights of the poor and needy."[30] Any hope offered must be real, tangible, substantial, and meaningful.

I'm certain that many of you have experienced this expression of faith in action in your own community, and like some of you, I've been extremely fortunate in that I have taken multiple short-term mission trips in the United States and around the globe. These trips are designed to offer tangible hope by helping in the areas of disaster relief and long-term challenges like affordable housing, clean water, food, orphan care, and medical attention. These trips have changed not only my life but also the lives of those with whom I have traveled. So it seems as if crazy sheep walk in the footsteps of the Crazy

Shepherd by handing out cold cups of water (a catchall phrase describing acts of compassion and mercy). Like Jesus, their compassionate service to others often begins with addressing both physical and felt needs: serving the poor, the homeless, the orphaned, and widowed, as well as anyone else who finds themselves on the short side of life. They lead with compassion; it's what crazy sheep do.

But upon further reflection, there is a crazy twist in that the idea of compassionately serving the poor, the homeless, and those who live on the fringe of hope is not all that crazy anymore. There are hundreds if not thousands of incredible humanitarian organizations that do the same thing, and they do so with love and excellence. While it was rare or even unheard of in the first century, today it is extremely popular for organizations and companies both large and small to become involved in their community as they reach out to those who have less. Compassion, local and global, is rising to the surface. It's a beautiful picture.

So what then makes the compassion work of crazy sheep any different than theirs? What's so crazy about doing something that's being done by more people and organizations than we can count? No doubt, we need to appreciate and honor the work of the aforementioned groups; it is much needed in this hurting world, and my hat is off to all of them. They are doing a great service to our community and world, and we should make sure they know how much we appreciate their incredible commitment and sacrifice. However if you stop and think back to Solomon's tree of life and the two-sided coin of hope, addressing physical and felt needs alone can short-change the depth of the hope that people also need. If we stop at handing out that cold cup of water and go no further, we're missing something. If this is the only hope we're offering, it will at some point fade away. While this may not be hope deferred, it can be hope short-lived. We will never meet the entirety of everyone's physical and felt needs. They never go away. Yes, we live in an unfair and unjust world, and we must work diligently at regularly offering that cold cup of water, but at the same time, there is something much deeper at stake: the eternal hope that never fades, never spoils, nor can it be ever be taken away. The other side of hope's coin, the eternal side, must not be set aside nor forgotten.

This is what can truly make all the difference in this profoundly hurting world. It's a tough subject in our work of compassion. I guess this is why it's so crazy. But Peter, one of Christ's craziest followers, brings it together this way:

> In your hearts revere Christ as Lord. Always be prepared to give an answer to everyone who asks you to give the reason for the hope that you have. But do this with gentleness and respect...[31]

In other words, as crazy sheep are handing out that cold cup of water, they would do well to politely and respectfully share the why behind the what, the reason that they care so deeply, the heart behind all that they do, and the Person for whom they lead with compassion: Jesus. This Crazy Shepherd, who offered tangible hope for the here and now by addressing physical and emotional needs, is also the only true hope for the hereafter, our eternal life. While sharing both sides of hope's coin may seem crazy and difficult at times, it's easier than you may think, and it often starts with a simple prayer.

His name was Robert but most simply called him Bob. He and his wife had two girls, and early in their lives Bob owned his own business with his father. Bob was a hard-working guy and a former navy Seabee in World War II (he helped prepare the way for soldiers to invade various islands in the Pacific theater). He was a good father and in many ways spoiled the girls, but it was his way of expressing the depth of his love for them. This was all well and good until his father cheated him out of the family business, and this was when the wheels began to fall off the wagon. Bob and his wife became heavy drinkers, and this would take its toll on the entire family for years to come.

Bob was an incredibly fun-loving man who enjoyed a good party with his family, neighbors, and friends. It was in this outgoing dynamic where he hid the deeper issues of his heart and soul. Over time, as his two girls became adults, his heavy drinking began to chip away at their relationship. He was at times obnoxious, and his anger at the loss of his business often pushed him to bitterness. While he never lashed out at his girls, when drunk he was extremely difficult to deal with. It became much worse when his wife died of emphysema in her late fifties, and within months he quickly latched on to someone else. By now his relationship with his two girls was extremely stressed. Within the next two years, Bob was diagnosed with lung cancer and as such needed special care, so he moved in with his youngest daughter. It was while he lived with her that he began his chemo and radiation treatments. She would care for him, attend to his needs, take him to various doctor appointments, often bath him, and dress him. But the years of accumulated anger, disappointment, and bitterness lingered in the background.

Enter Edith. While Bob was living with his youngest daughter and receiving his cancer treatments, Edith would visit him regularly. She would stop by a few times a week to help care for him and just talk with him for a few hours. They would laugh together and remember what life was like during and after the war (Edith was his age and the mother in law of his youngest daughter). This went on for months, and after every visit, Edith would politely ask how she could pray for him, and he always shared a few needs. However, over the course of time with Edith, Bob found himself falling in love with the Jesus he never knew before, and his demeanor began to change. It was during this time when he and youngest daughter began to talk about the deeper sides of life, and over the ensuing months, the wounds of the past forty years began to slowly heal. For the first time in many years, they truly enjoyed each other's company through their laughter and their tears. A year later, even though he passed while living with his daughter, she would often look back at those months with him as an unexpected and very welcomed gift from God. It all began with Edith's offer of a cold cup of water and a simple prayer. I know this story to be true; Edith was my mother, and Bob was my father-in-law. While he lived with my wife and I, Bob became a different man. He experienced a tangible hope for both the present as well as the eternal. It was a sight to behold. There are many stories like this one; it's only one example of two-sided hope. The manner by which crazy sheep share this hope found only in the Crazy Shepherd has countless flavors and expressions. What worked for my mom, and now works for me, may not necessarily work for you. It's up to you to figure out the best way to express this hope.

Looking back over the years, I think our lives are much like a movie, a grandiose story with many scenes unfolding over the course of our lives. Like my favorite western, our story too is one of deep and at times unexpected friendships that carry tremendous weight. And as each chapter unfolds, we meet people almost every day that others seem to ignore and overlook, people who are down and out, live on the wrong side of life, caught up in a whirlwind of setbacks, having a really bad week, or, like Doc Holiday, are sometimes very hard to love. Offering them a cold cup of water that is also filled with the fervent prayers of forgiveness and laced with a hope for eternity can go a long way in removing the walls that keep us apart. True, some will politely say no thanks, but some will eagerly say yes. As we are handing out that cold cup of water, wouldn't it be amazing to hear these words: *You're the only human being who ever gave me hope.*

This two-sided coin of hope, in all of its depth and richness, is for you, as well as for those you know. You too can offer that cold cup of water and a simple prayer, and in doing so you offer a tangible hope for both the present and the eternal. It's not as hard as you may think. People need you more than you may know.

Crazy hope, two sides of the same majestic coin; it's the way of crazy sheep.

CHAPTER 4   CRAZY DREAMERS AND DREAM-MAKERS | *Moving Beyond the Things That Can Hold You Back*

Most of us grow up with a deep desire to live the American dream, or as Star Trek's Spock would say to Captain Kirk, "Live long and prosper." This is what most us want in life: to do well, to dream big, to live long, to raise our families, and retire early so we can enjoy our grandchildren and the prosperous life that we've worked hard to attain. It's the American dream, and it doesn't seem like it's too much to ask. But then, as we all know, life gets in the way. The road to living our dreams sometimes gets obstructed with roadblocks. There are obstacles and challenges to overcome, and often we settle down and face the so-called realities of life. We now have duties, obligations, debts, and responsibilities. There are people who now depend on us, and so our deepest dreams are relegated to the attic with the rest of our memorabilia. Sound familiar?

Additionally in the pursuit of our dreams, we occasionally bump into people who for whatever reason want to squash our dreams and the deepest longings that come with them. It's difficult to rationalize, but when dreamers dream, they often times find themselves fighting off those who think they are crazy, unrealistic, overreaching, ill equipped, unqualified, or unrealistic in the size or scope of their dreams. Why some people try to keep dreamers from dreaming is anyone's guess. Maybe it's fear, jealousy, or personal agenda.

It is here that I'm reminded of *October Sky*, a movie based on the true story of Homer Hickam, a young boy who had larger-than-life dreams, but around every corner there were those who wanted to keep him in his place. One night as he was looking up at the October sky, Homer, played by Jake Gyllenhaal, notices the Russian satellite (Sputnik) orbiting the earth, and it inspires him to build a rocket that will help him explore and dig deeper into outer space. Overcoming a poor education, a difficult father, a less than encouraging school principal, and many others who thought he was being unrealistic, Homer begins to design and build his own rockets. With the help of a teacher, he recruits his friends, called the Rocket Boys, and in the midst of those who attempted to steal his dreams, and after many failures, he and the Rocket Boys ultimately go on to win regional and national science awards. Eventually Homer becomes a research scientist with NASA. It's an inspiring true story.[32] What makes this movie worth watching is that you catch a glimpse of those who dream and those who help those dreams come true, and as you will see, they are inseparable.

Speaking of great movies, have you ever watched *The Ten Commandments* by Cecil B. De Mill? It's the story of Moses and how he manages to help a few million Hebrews escape four hundred years of Egyptian slavery. I don't know how you could miss it; it's on TV every Easter. If you've never heard of Moses and his grand adventures, you could set aside a few weeks and read about him in the book of Exodus, or if you are short on time like the rest of us, you could always take a few hours, grab a bag of popcorn, and watch the movie. Like most movies it's not a perfect reflection of the book, but it is a classic and gets you close enough for the topic that we need to review. I'm all for shortcuts, and by now you should know how much I love a good movie. So don't panic; you can always read the book of Exodus later. I can already hear the complaints by the *religious others*.[33]

Why do I bring up Moses? His story will help us capture the nature of the kind of dreams we need to talk about, where they come from, who dreams them, and how their dreams unfold. Moses wasn't by nature a dreamer, but if we pay close attention, we can learn much from him. Assuming that you are at least somewhat familiar with the story, let's review what we can learn from this reluctant dreamer.

Dreamers and Dream-Makers

Upon escaping the grip of the Pharaoh in Egypt, if it were not for his one to two million followers, Moses the dreamer may have been just another aimless desert wanderer—alone in the wilderness with no one following. In other words, dreamers typically don't get very far without people following them. Followers are the dream-makers that dreamers need. Actually I can't think of any dreamers who didn't desperately need dream-makers by their side, for without them, dreams are rarely, if ever, realized in full. While dreamers are typically the catalyst behind every worthwhile endeavor, dream-makers are what make the dreamer's dreams come to fruition, and the art of dream-making has been called the art of followership. The church, or any organization for that matter, needs first-rate followers, crazy dream-makers who can complement and support crazy dreamers.

Crazy dream-makers actually have more influence than they usually acknowledge and are dedicated to carrying out the mission and purpose of the organization. Furthermore, at their core is the platform of solid interpersonal relationships with both God and others. Indeed, crazy dream-makers with their unique skills and abilities are just as critical to the success of the organization as crazy dreamers, and it is fair to have high expectations of both. In short, both are indispensable. It can be said that crazy dream-makers are leaders in their own right. They are mission critical to the success of your church or ministry. They are the ones who make *vision a reality*. They are the ones who will help dreamers realize their ministry dreams. It is here that I offer the following brief summary:

- Crazy dream-makers are people of authenticity and community; they refuse to do life alone.

- Crazy dream-makers are people with a high degree of integrity and personal character.

- Crazy dream-makers are people of passion, a passion that is driven by their deep desire to serve Christ.

- Crazy dream-makers are people of both personal and corporate vision, mission, and purpose.

- Crazy dream-makers are people with a set of personal values, one of which is carrying the towel of a humble servant.

It is with a bunch of crazy, sold-out dream-makers that the Crazy Shepherd launched the single largest dream in human history: the church. So being a crazy dream-maker isn't as insignificant as you may think.

Crazy Ordinary

In our prevailing culture, we're led to believe that only the exceptionally gifted and talented can make it really big in life. We live in a culture where people will do most anything to attain his or her fifteen minutes of fame. All you need to do is watch *America's Got Talent, American Idol,* or *The Voice.* I'm not suggesting that these shows are not worth watching, but you have to admit: they have propagated a culture that suggests only the talented few can make it big. The rest of us are therefore destined to live in the world of ordinary, or so the story goes. Not that long ago, there was a TV commercial poking fun at those who find themselves in middle management, those who see themselves as average, and those who find themselves in ordinary jobs living an ordinary life. The underlying message of the commercial was that being ordinary could be boring! It's an unfortunate commentary, don't you think?

When you read (or watch) the story of Moses, you will notice that early on he often complained to God that he lacked the necessary skills and abilities that are required when leading more than a million people out of Egypt. In his opinion, he wasn't properly equipped. He had a problem speaking to others and lacked the organizational skills that it would take to get things moving in the right direction. He was just an ordinary guy, someone destined to be average. It's funny in one sense because when people think you are just an ordinary, run-of-the-mill person, they have a tendency to write you off, and this is when you can sneak in under the radar. For example, take a look at how the religious leaders viewed the early followers of the Crazy Shepherd.

> When they saw the courage of Peter and John and realized that they were unschooled, ordinary men, they were astonished and they took note that these men had been with Jesus.[34]

These guys who flew under the radar of said religious leaders went on to launch a movement of cosmic proportions, and Jesus could have chosen anyone he wanted. He could have done the job himself, but it was with those who were seen as ordinary and unschooled that he rallied to fulfill his dreams. It's the nature of the Dream-giver.

One of the most telling verses of how Christ views those who have been relegated to living in the back stage of life is found in Matthew 5:1-9. In Christian circles, this section is called the Sermon on the Mount, or the Beatitudes. What these verses describe is the very nature of those whom Jesus was most interested in at the time, those the religious leaders had written off because of a less-than-stellar life, social status, upbringing, religious heritage, marital status, messed-up life, broken family, or meager education level. The people who gathered on the side of the mountain to whom Jesus was referring were those who were considered unqualified and unworthy of Kingdom work or even an entrance into that Kingdom. They were the poor in spirit, the ones who mourn, the meek at heart, the merciful, the peacemakers, and those who simply hungered for a right standing in the eyes of God. What Jesus was teaching his disciples is that he sees those sitting on the mountainside differently. However, in the hearts and minds of those who were running the religious show, those who considered themselves more qualified and better equipped to lead the Temple, they were the ones who determined who was in and who was out. As it relates to those on the mountainside, N. T. Wright shares the following:

> The Sermon on the Mount is a call to Jesus' followers to take up their vocation as light to the world, as salt to the earth—in other words, as people through whom Jesus' kingdom vision is to become a reality...the work of the kingdom, in fact, is summed up pretty well in those Beatitudes. When God wants to change the world, he doesn't send in the tanks. He sends in the meek, the mourners, those who are hungry and thirsty for God's justice, the peacemakers, and so on.[35]

Please don't get me wrong; those who are profoundly talented and extremely gifted make a tremendous impact in this world, and the majority of them have worked extremely hard to get where they are. There is nothing more enjoyable than listening to a gifted vocalist, watching a great performer, or reaping the health benefits of a gifted research scientist. We thank God for them. The Crazy Shepherd, however, also believes deeply in ordinary people like us, no big surprise here. In other words, dreaming and dream-making aren't reserved for the profoundly gifted, the exceptionally well spoken, or the extremely talented. Crazy ordinary. What a concept. As it turns out, there is tremendous power and great satisfaction in being *crazy ordinary*.

The Necessity of Failure

When Moses finally got his act together and listened to God, he returned to Egypt. He then demanded that Pharaoh release his fellow Hebrews, and he thought a miracle would do the trick. With great fanfare (at least in the movie), using his shepherd's staff, he miraculously turned it into a snake. The people were shocked and amazed at the great power of Moses, but Pharaoh simply called upon his magicians to do the same. Moses, it seems, had failed.

The same happened when Moses returned and turned water from the Nile River into blood. Again Pharaoh was less than impressed. He saw Moses as a failure, weak, and ineffective. When you read the rest of the story, however, you realize that God had bigger ideas. He knew that it would take further convincing to force Pharaoh's hand.

If we're not careful, we too can fall into the trap of viewing our own failures as a sign of weakness. After all, who among us likes to fail? It is as though failure is bad. But you know what's coming: the Crazy Shepherd thinks differently. Failure can be a catalyst that moves us forward with our larger-than-life dreams. Some would say that failures are a necessary part of realizing our dreams. After all, as the old saying goes, if it were easy, anyone could do it. Sadly, in my experience, some people are unwilling to navigate the rough waters of failure, be they personal, relational, or otherwise. It's simply much easier to walk away and move on. This is an unfortunate commentary on life, and those who do walk away often miss something. Their dreams, which at one time excited their heart and soul, can actually be realized in full if they just press on. Marching steadfastly through our failures takes hard work, determination, sacrifice, endless review, and communication. Persistence means never losing sight of what can be, sometimes digging through the rubble of life, and surrounding yourself with those priceless dream-makers who simply won't let you quit. In other words, our failures are simply the necessary and sometimes heart-wrenching stepping-stones, which, if we're persistent, can lead us to seeing our deepest dreams become a reality. There is great power in failure, and if you stop and think about it, we're in good company.

On the day before the resurrection of Christ, the disciples were in disarray. They were beyond confused, heartbroken, and all appeared to be lost. They had followed Jesus for three years, and now it seemed as if their plan had failed miserably. Furthermore the religious leaders and the

Roman officials happily agreed: the cross was a failure. Well, yes and no. To the necessity of failure, John Ortberg makes the following extraordinary observation:

The response to the resurrection on the first Easter the Gospels consistently include fear. In fact, people were more afraid after the resurrection than they were before. And none of the Gospel accounts have Jesus or the angels saying, "Now you don't have to worry about dying anymore." What Jesus does say to his followers is that there is work to be done. In effect, "The cross didn't stick. Their plan to stop my movement didn't work. It's going to go on. Matter of fact, my plan to love even your enemies, to be willing to sacrifice, suffer, and even die for the sake of love has been vindicated by my Father. They're really going to be ticked off now. Pilate and the chief priests have already plotted to squelch this news. They are furious. They are desperate. I'm leaving now. So you go, you women, you disciples. Tell them all that the cross failed, Caesar failed, Pilate failed, the chief priests failed. Now they have you to contend with."[36]

Once again, there is power in what some perceive as failure. Kind of crazy cool, don't you think? How have you handled your failures? If they have pushed you out of the game, maybe it's time for you to learn from them and jump back in the mix. After all, when you invite the Crazy Shepherd into your life and let him guide you, the world will have you to contend with.

Your Dreams Are Too Small

Moses would have been fine living in Goshen (this is where he went when he fled Egypt). Upon arriving there his mind was on nothing more than surviving, and having done so, he was satisfied with life. It was an early rendition of the American dream. After all, there he had a good wife, an honorable profession, and a solid family. He had all that he really needed. If you watched the whole movie (or read the whole book), however, you know that God had other plans. God sparked a thread of deep curiosity in Moses's heart and mind.

I remember it as if it was yesterday. One of my older brothers asked me what I wanted to do after high school, so I told him that I wanted to become an electrician. His response shocked me, and I was fairly certain he was off his rocker. He said to me, "Ron, becoming an electrician is a great idea. It can be a solid career. However, why don't you take some college classes that will someday help you own the electrical company?" He left it at that. In essence my brother was trying to tell me that while my dream of being an electrician was really good, it was entirely possible that my dream was too small. By the way, I'm not the only one who lived in the comfort of my so-called small dreams. You need look no further than a fisherman by the name of Peter. Let's take a look.

One day as Jesus was preaching on the shore of the Sea of Galilee, great crowds pressed in on him to listen to the word of God. He noticed two empty boats at the water's edge, for the fishermen had left them and were washing their nets. Stepping into one of the boats, Jesus asked Simon, its owner, to push it out into the water. So he sat in the boat and taught the crowds from there. When he had finished speaking, he said to Simon, "Now go out where it is deeper, and let down your nets to catch some fish." "Master," Simon replied, "we worked hard all last night and didn't catch a thing. But if you say so, I'll let the nets down again." And this time their nets were so full of fish they began to tear! A shout for help brought their partners in the other boat, and soon both boats were filled with fish and on the verge of sinking.

When Simon Peter realized what had happened, he fell to his knees before Jesus and said, "Oh, Lord, please leave me—I'm too much of a sinner to be around you." For he was awestruck by the number of fish they had caught, as were the others with him. His partners, James and John, the sons of Zebedee, were also amazed. Jesus replied to Simon, "Don't be afraid! From now on you'll be fishing for people!" And as soon as they landed, they left everything and followed Jesus.[37]

There are many great lessons and insights in this story, and I think one of them is found in the underlying message that Jesus was offering to Peter. It's as if Jesus was saying, "Peter, someday you will stop fishing for just fish. The 'Peter and Andrew Fishing Company' is great, but, Peter, your dreams are too small. Someday, you and your brother will be fishing for men and women who will take your dreams to places you've never thought possible." While he didn't recognize it at the time, this sometimes-overbearing fisherman would help start a movement of global and cultural change, a movement of historical proportions, a movement called the church. So if your dream is to simply live the American dream, then maybe—just maybe—your dream is too small. Perhaps it's time for you to lock arms with other crazy sheep and let the Crazy Shepherd breathe new life (and a few larger-than-your-own dreams that come with it) back into your heart, mind, and soul. Kingdom dreams are what make you crazy!

Dreamers and dream-makers, larger-than-life dreams, the power of being ordinary, and the pleasure of failure. This is the way of crazy sheep. Ready to get crazy yet? Ready to dream crazy dreams of what can be? Ready to take your *ordinariness* to an all-time high? Ready to become a crazy dream-maker? If so, then welcome to the gang of crazies.

Well not so fast. Before you go running out the door with a newfound fervor and zeal, there is a crazy twist that we need to examine. It's great to have dreams, visions of what can be and what you want to accomplish in life; it's what makes life worth living. But just as it was with handing out that cold cup of water, what is it that makes the dreams of crazy sheep any different from the dreams of anyone else? Is it simply because they follow the Crazy Shepherd, or is there something more to it? To answer these questions, we must explore the nature of who, why, and what is behind the dreams and dream-making of those who follow Christ. For it is here that we can begin to catch a glimpse of a difference. Before we get started, however, there is one thing I need to make perfectly clear. The difference we're going to examine is not an exercise in determining who has better dreams or which dream-maker is immersed in a more noble cause. Again, dreamers and dream-makers, wherever they are found, add treasured value to the totality of life. So, with that being said, I would like to examine dreams that revolve around the holistic needs of others.

The Nature of Who: The Crazy Dream-Giver

Have you ever wondered who or what is behind the dreams and visions people have? What is the source of their dreams? Who is it that motivates dreamers and dream-makers? What was it that sparked that thread of curiosity in the mind and heart of Moses? Was it a person, a circumstance, or an event? I'm sure that to some degree all three play a role, but more often than not, it is a *who* that stands behind the dreams of crazy sheep. For example, what was it that prompted Richard Stearns to set aside his incredible career at Lenox, the American gift and tableware company, and take a job at World Vision? Or what was behind Cicely Saunders's dreams of what would become hospice, a place for terminally ill patients who were systematically ignored by the medical profession? Do some of your own research, and look into the history of Samaritan's Purse, Compassion International, the Salvation Army, and the Red Cross. In doing so you'll see a common thread behind those who founded these extraordinary organizations. In each of the aforementioned examples, it was their profound faith in Christ that moved them to stand up to injustice, to take bold and unprecedented steps for those who could no longer fend for themselves, and to intervene at all costs to right a wrong and set a sustainable path for others to follow. It was the Crazy Shepherd who pushed them to pursue crazy dreams, and herein rests a fundamental difference between crazy sheep and most everyone else.

Crazy dreamers and crazy dream-makers look to Christ for their dreams. What makes these dreams different is that they typically revolve around the emotional, physical, and spiritual needs of others, those who have lost hope and live on the fringes of life by no fault of their own. And it is in the midst of this that we need to hearken back to that cold cup of water and the *tree of life*. Because if you recall, the hope that is being offered is a two-sided coin, hope for the here and now as well as hope for the eternal. This is at the very core of crazy dreamers and crazy dream-makers. Furthermore it was both sides of hope's coin that motivated the heart of the Crazy Shepherd, and as such, he is the one behind our crazy dreams. He is the Crazy Dream-giver, and in him rests all the difference.

The Nature of Why: An Act of Worship

At the know-it-all age of sixteen, I found myself at a church revival service in the middle of a rather energetic and engaging time of musical worship when all of a sudden the worship leader jumped in and proclaimed, "Wow, this must be what it's going to be like in heaven!" Everyone cheered except me. I remember thinking, *Oh, good, organs and wooden pews in heaven—just what I need.* If you have read *The Religion of Jesus*, you know that I didn't have the best attitude about church, Christianity, or religion at that age. The words *shallow* and *narrow-minded* come to mind.

Today we still have worship services, worship leaders, and some churches have directors of worship arts. In most churches the order of service on any given Sunday is categorized into a time of worship, a time for the Word of God, a time of offering, and a time of prayer, just to name a few. You get the picture. Could it be that over the years we've managed to put worship into a category by itself? Is it possible that we have limited the idea of worship to music and singing, and in doing so, have we unintentionally limited the essence of what it means to worship? Is it possible that worship was intended to be much more holistic, encompassing all areas of life, and find its expression in most everything we do? In *Simply Jesus: A New Vision of Who He Was, What He Did, and Why It Matters*, N. T. Wright speaks to the nature of worship.

> All kingdom work is rooted in worship. Or, to put it the other way around, worshipping the God we see at work in Jesus is the most political-ly charged act we can ever perform. Christian worship declares that Jesus is Lord and that therefore, by strong implication, nobody else is. What's more, it doesn't just declare it as something to be believed, like the fact that the sun is hot or the sea wet. It commits the worshipper to allegiance, to following this Jesus, to being shaped and directed by him. Worshipping the God we see in Jesus orients our whole being, our imagination, our will, our hopes, and our fears.[38]

This is an extremely important discussion because deep beneath our God-given dreams and dream-making rests the nature of why we long to live them out. For pursuing our God-given crazy dreams, and gathering a crew of crazy dream-makers to guide us along the way, is an expression of worship—one among many. Furthermore in worship, regardless of how it is expressed, you may also discover the fine art of humble service to the King of kings, and subsequently, to those who find themselves on the short end of love and their own ever-so-fleeting dreams of what life can be. Worship is all-encompassing, and this most assuredly includes dreaming and dream-making.

The Nature of Where: Wherever You Find Yourself

There was a time in our church history when traveling preachers and evangelists would gather the young and the not-so-young to share the Good News of Jesus Christ. Typically at some point toward the end of their message, they would begin talking about going into the mission field. With great energy and fanfare, they would look to the final instructions of the Crazy Shepherd.

> Jesus came and told his disciples, "I have been given all authority in heaven and on earth. Therefore, go and make disciples of all the nations, baptizing them in the name of the Father and the Son and the Holy Spirit. Teach these new disciples to obey all the commands I have given you. And be sure of this: I am with you always, even to the end of the age."[39]

They would point to the word *go*, and from here they would invite everyone in the crowd to obey the words of Jesus and *go* into the world as missionaries or evangelists like themselves. The mood was emotional and the calling was straightforward. *Go!* I remember these meetings. As a young man, I sat in on a few. The challenge in my mind was that I didn't want to become a missionary or anything like one. I had other plans. So like many others in the crowd, I left feeling rather guilty of not wanting to fulfill what Christians call the Great Commission. I didn't want to *go!*

Ironically, I did find my way to becoming a pastor later in life, but the idea of being pushed into bypassing my own plans and going into the mission field never sat well with me. It wasn't until I began studying the nature of language and grammar that I found some sense of relief, and in many ways it took the pressure off. In Matthew 28:19, the word *go* is not the verb of the sentence. In other words, it is not the point, or the action item, that Jesus was trying to make. The verb is actually *make disciples* (teaching and helping people become students and fellow crazy followers of Christ). While the idea of making disciples could be a book on its own, the point of our discussion is on the word *go*. In the context of this verse, *go* is actually a participle, and as such, it has a profoundly different meaning. In effect, what Jesus was saying is *as you go*. In other words, *as you go* in your life, whether you are a preacher, a lawyer, a homemaker, a CEO, a grocery clerk, or an electrician, make disciples of those you meet. When I figured this out, all of the aforementioned pressures evaporated, and I finally realized that it was OK to become whatever I wanted to become, and wherever I found myself, I could still do my best to fulfill the great mission of the Crazy Shepherd. And I could do so in the familiarity of my own zip code.

The same is true for you. Wherever you find yourself, you can still dream crazy dreams or become a crazy dream-maker—no pressure here. With this in mind, it's important to note that God-directed dreams are more diverse than there are crazy sheep who dream them. They come in many shapes and sizes. It's the nature of the Dream-giver, and there are no limits to those dreams. Given my personal bent toward reaching out to those who find themselves on the less fortunate side of life, however, I have a few questions. Who will be the next crazy dreamer who will dream of a way to address the educational challenges facing our inner-city kids, and if there is a dreamer who has already done so, who will be the dream-makers who rally alongside them? In the spirit of the Dream-giver and the dreamers he inspires, the same question can be asked of:

- Figuring out new ways to address the ever-present loneliness of our senior citizens who are left to fend for themselves.

- Developing the next interactive and innovative curriculum that will take our kids into the crazy world of life and faith in the Dream-giver.

- Re-visioning and reshaping the methods by which we address the fractured lives of abused and orphaned children.

- Creating a safe places where lifelong caregivers can go to relax and refuel.

- Formulating innovative ways to provide tangible respite care for families with children who have special needs.

The above list goes on and on, and we are only limited by our own imagination. But whether your dreams of what can be are local, regional, national, or global, it matters not. It matters deeply, however, to the one who will benefit from your dreams and dream-making. After all, the Crazy Shepherd was just as concerned for the one as he was concerned for the many, wherever they may be.

It is off-the-charts thrilling to be crazy dreamers and crazy dream-makers who simply wake up every morning with a desire to follow in the footsteps of the Crazy Shepherd; this is what this book is all about. We could easily move on from this topic, but it is here that we need to stop and dig just a bit deeper. There is one more twist, and this one hits home.

When It All Falls Down

There are times in life when something happens that causes the sum of our hopes and dreams to come crashing down. I'm not talking about the aforementioned failures or setbacks. I'm talking about a level of personal loss that is beyond what we can control. There are times when we are blindsided by the tragedies of life and circumstance. It's not fair, but they are very real. The death of a spouse, the loss of a child, a painful divorce, tragic accidents, or events that extinguish the lives of those we hold do dear, each in their own way can take a horrible toll on our lives, and the dreams that were once so vibrant can come crashing down in an instant. So there we sit. I actually had second thoughts about including this part in the book, but there is a part of me that thinks if you want to truly walk in the crazy footsteps of Jesus, you have to sometimes find a way to wade through the ugly realities of this life. So in my mind, not mentioning this would be dishonest and inauthentic, and not bringing it up would miss the deeper point of it all (we will dig a bit deeper in the next chapter).

It's no secret. At times life is excruciatingly hard, and rediscovering your hopes and dreams is sometimes even harder. In times like these, when you have experienced the shattering of your deepest dreams and the tender hopes that come with them, you can find yourself lost and drifting away. Somewhere between grief and loneliness, you frequently find yourself asking, Is there a place for me? Is there someone who can help hold my life together? Is there someone who truly understands? Will I ever make it through the next day? Will I ever dream again? Will the hope that I once held so dear ever find its way back to the surface? There are no easy answers to these extremely difficult and sometimes unanswerable questions. I've been there. I get it. My world, my hopes, and my dreams all came crashing down on at 9:35 p.m., Thursday, July 7, 2011, when my precious wife and best friend unexpectedly passed. There is a battery-powered clock in my kitchen that reads 9:35, and I removed the batteries as a reminder of when my life changed forever. It's never easy. It never goes away. My personal experience, however, has also taught me that we should never give up. Never!

While challenging days will continue to surface, and it will seem as if it's a long way off, it is quite possible that you will learn how to dream again, and along the path of never giving up, new dreams may emerge, ones that you never saw coming or thought you would ever have. This book is an example of how dreams can find their way to the surface again. It wasn't until after my wife's death that I started writing. So as it turns out, the Crazy Shepherd is always up to something, and my deepest hope is that by the time you finish this book, you'll see that all is not lost when it all falls down before your very eyes. Chapter 6, The Crazy Life, offers some personal insights as to how one begins to slowly move forward. I know, when you're hurting, this kind of thinking sounds crazy, but I'm not the one making the promise. It is the Crazy Shepherd.

The Lord is close to the broken hearted and saves those who are crushed in spirit. Come to me, all of you who are weary and carry heavy burdens, and I will give you rest. Take my yoke upon you. Let me teach you, because I am humble and gentle at heart, and you will find rest for your souls.[40]

Crazy dreams and dream-making, and moving beyond the things that can hold you back. It is possible. Never give up. This is the way of the Crazy Shepherd, and as such, it is also the way of his crazy sheep.

CHAPTER 5 CRAZY PEACE | *Moving Beyond Your Secret Loneliness*

During the summer of 1998, my wife and I decided it was time for us to take another short-term mission trip. We had been on trips to the Dominican Republic in previous years, but she had to take a break because of her health. So over the course of two months, since she was feeling better, we prayed about this trip and talked about it with a few good friends. There was no question in our minds that it was the right time to go, and God was behind it all, so we decided to take a group to Mexico and help a friend with his new ministry. The way we described it to our supporters is that we were prayed up, packed up, and ready to go. In the three years preceding this trip, because of some complications and side affects of lupus, my wife had both of her hips replaced. By the time we had decided to go on another trip, however, she was back on her feet and ready to serve the children of Reynosa, Mexico. We were thoroughly convinced that all would be fine. After all, we were serving the God of promise.

There were eight of us who left for Mexico on a Saturday, and when we arrived at the airport, we were met by our good friends George and Jan. That evening after dinner, we mapped out our plans for the week, prayed as a group for good health and safety, sang a few songs together, and then retired for the night. The next morning we decided to go to the village where we would be working. We visited the kids and families with whom we would be interacting throughout the coming week. It was thrilling to see the excitement of the kids and the smiles on the faces of two families who would receive a new house. It was a great day, and our group was more than ready to get started the next morning. We went back to the camp, got cleaned up, and gathered around a large round table for dinner. While we were eating and talking about the next day, however, our world of excitement and anticipation evaporated in an instant. As she was sitting in her chair enjoying the food and conversation, my wife's left hip dislocated without warning. In a matter of seconds she was in extreme pain, and I vividly remember looking at her and seeing a depth of frustration and agony in her eyes that is hard to describe. All of our hopes and dreams of a successful mission trip came crashing down. In a matter of mere moments, all of our prayers seemed like a waste of time, all of our preparation seemed senseless, and in my mind, all the promises that God had made became empty, null, and void.

Bonnie was more than heart broken; I was more than angry. As George, Jan, the crew, and I gathered around her and tried to make her comfortable, I couldn't take it anymore. She and I had been down this path before, but all indications were that this trip was supposed to be different. Furious at my very core, I ran out of the side door into a farmer's field and began to look for rocks so I could throw them at God. One of the young men on our team came running out to console me, but I warned him that he had better go back into the building because he wouldn't like what he was about to see. So I picked up as many rocks as I could find and threw them into air, aiming for God; he was no friend of mine. How dare he let my wife down and disappoint her so. After my rock-throwing tirade, we loaded Bonnie into the van and headed back to the border so we could take her to a hospital in the States. The trip seemed long, and she was in trouble. After a few hours, we found a hospital and rushed her into the emergency room. Over the course of the next few days, the doctors finally resolved the dislocation, and thanks to a friend back in Michigan who had air shipped us Bonnie's leg brace, we began the long, exasperating, and disappointing drive back home. Our dear and trusted friend Pam, who was on the trip with us, came along so she could help with the driving and the care of my wife. Pam's assistance was priceless, but it would be the last international mission trip my wife would take.[41]

Have you ever been so disappointed with God that you began to demand answers? Have you ever been so angry with God that you wanted to throw rocks at him? If so, welcome to the real world, where some answers are fleeting, and it can be a very lonely place.

As I mentioned in previous chapter, we need to climb further into the rabbit hole, and we begin by talking about the deeper side of our life as crazy followers of Christ. It is here that many will think we are more than just different; they will think that we have possibly lost touch with reality, that we swim against the current of cultural trends and against the streams of reason. What we're going to talk about is far from easy, and it may take some time to get there, but what else would you expect from the Crazy Shepherd?

Finding Peace from the Outside In: Living Life with a Trusted Friend

So much has been written about *doing life* with others that I'm afraid to attempt an explanation of it and how it affects our lives. There may be more books, websites, study guides, seminars, workshops, and group life experts than there are small groups in the known universe. Of course I'm only joking, but you have to admit, there has been an enormous amount of research and discussion on the topic, and as such, I suspect the vast majority of us are fully aware that we are indeed social creatures. We were built to interact with each other on an ongoing basis, and whether we realize it or not, how it plays out in our lives is something we work through each and every day. In other words, *doing life* together is an unavoidable dynamic of everyday life. By design of the One who created us, our interaction with others, when viewed through the proper lens, can help us dig deeper into the peace that God offers and how that peace finds its way into the deepest recesses of our heart and soul. Solomon was well aware of this when he offered the following counterintuitive advice:

Wounds from a friend can be trusted, but an enemy multiplies kisses. Perfume and incense bring joy to the heart, and the pleasantness of a friend springs from their heartfelt advice. Gracious words are a honeycomb, sweet to the soul and healing to the bones.[42]

Wounds from a friend can be trusted seems so very odd at first. Why would a friend wound another friend? Maybe the answer comes in the form of another question. Have you ever had someone tell you something you didn't really want to hear, but when all was said and done, you knew it was the right thing to do? Me too. This type of wound opens up the areas of life where we may be blind to our weaknesses, shortsighted as to our shortcomings, or unwilling to come to terms with our less-than-admirable motives. This type of friend is not afraid to challenge our thinking by lovingly telling us what most don't like hearing: the truth. Friends like this are desperately needed, and when we find one, they become irreplaceable. It is important to pay close attention to what Solomon said. *Wounds from a friend can be trusted.* Solomon is not talking merely about the idea of being *wounded* by a friend and the benefits therein but also about the *type* of friend that can be trusted.

At present I have around 450 Facebook friends, but there are only four or five who I would consider *trusted friends.* They are the ones who know me be better that I know myself. They have walked with me through success and failure, been side-by-side in pure joy and deepest sorrow, loved me when I was hard to love, and carried me when I could hardly stand on my own two feet. Trusted friends don't come and go. They don't leave you when you're hard to be with or when life gets messy. Nor do they walk away when life gets so difficult it seems as if all is lost. This may sound extremely trivial, but trusted friends rarely say, "Call me sometime." Instead they pick up the phone and call you. Trusted friends don't just *do life*; they *give life.* Many of us *do life,* but the deeper question is do we *give life.* Ask yourself, *Am I a friend who can be trusted? Am I a friend who gives life?*

Over time this counterintuitive way of life can sooth the heart and heal the soul, but it is up to each of us to seek it out and invite it in. The question isn't whether or not we choose to *do life together*, it's whether or not we *live life* in the company of a few trusted friends, for in doing so we can begin to experience true life change, not only in ourselves but also in those around us. Turning our backs on this vital component of life will more often than not leave us where we are: stuck in the middle of our secret loneliness. There is, however, one central dynamic that I would like to point out as it relates to trusting friendships, and I have found it exceedingly beneficial in my own quest to move beyond my secret loneliness.

The Most Pressing Challenge: The Fine Art of Listening

Have you ever had a conversation where you know that other person is totally distracted or uninterested? During conversations of this sort, you could say almost anything and the other person will simply wait and then share what was next on their mind. You could have told them that the other night you were abducted by alien life forms, taken to the planet Zargon, and then forced to eat things that smelled like old gym shorts, and the response would be something like, "Uh-uh. Did I tell you about my new job?" I'll bet you know exactly what I'm talking about. Some time ago a friend of mine and I invented a word: *bidostricate*. There is no such word, but we would use it when we knew someone wasn't listening. For example, if you and I were having a conversation and I knew that your mind was elsewhere, I might throw this out there: "The other day I was on my way to the post office when a UPS truck ran a red light and bidostricated the entire intersection." Your response might then be, "Bummer. Did I tell you that I just bought a new car?" It went right over your head; you were not actually listening. My wife thought using an invented word in that way was extremely rude. Maybe she was right, but it does illustrate a point.

There is a difference between listening and simply waiting for your turn to talk. Listening is much more than hearing words. It's the process of setting your world aside and allowing what others are saying to sink in. Listening sometimes involves the engagement of many of our senses: hearing, seeing, smelling, and touching. Listening is a lost art, and during a conversation, some of the best listeners rarely if ever talk about themselves. As mentioned in chapter 1, you can recognize them in an instant. As I see it, genuine listening involves three important dynamics: timing, patience, and empathy. *Timing* is it the right time and or the right place for your conversation. Has the other person had a bad day? Is there enough time to really get into it? Are you trying to talk to someone who is watching his or her favorite movie? (Guess who had a hard time listening while watching a movie?) Are you attempting to talk to someone who is already distracted? You get the idea. Listening and expecting someone else to do the same involves the right timing—timing is everything. *Patience* in this context means being willing to let the other person absorb what's being said and then letting them think it through for a while. Do you expect immediate answers or feedback? Do you offer answers without pondering the question or asking follow-up questions that dig a bit deeper? Are you able to walk away from the conversation, process it, and then find a time to get back into it? My counselor friend Gregg refers to this as being willing to call a *time out*, but not forgetting to also call a *time in*. Effective listening requires a great deal of patience.

The old saying that people need to know you care before they care what you know is as true today as it was when it was first written. But there is a difference between sympathy and empathy. Empathy can be defined as deeply understanding what someone else is feeling because you can in some way put yourself in his or her shoes; you can feel their pain or sorrow deep inside your own heart and soul. Sympathy, however, is acknowledging a person's emotional hardships and doing your best to provide some level of comfort and assurance.

Empathy is one of three key ingredients to effective listening. In my experience most people aren't looking for your answers to their situation; they simply need to be heard by someone with an empathetic nonjudgmental ear.

Timing, patience, and empathy are some of the tools of effective listening, and using them properly requires practice. When we love others as ourselves, we're simply loving them in the same way we ourselves would love to be loved, and in doing so, we will love others with a high degree of integrity (i.e., a soundness of character or structure). Remember that it's not the character and nature of the ones being loved, it's the character and nature of the ones doing the loving *and listening*. It's easier to truly love others this way because we know what it sounds like and how it should feel, and there is a profound richness in this kind of love. Again, it is the birthplace of empathy, and it is here that the fine art of listening can be rediscovered. If you can cross the bridge from merely hearing into listening without judgment, you will help others find their way toward crazy peace.

Without question, living life with a trusted friend or two plays a larger-than-life role in the process by which we can move beyond our secret loneliness, recapture our shattered dreams, and begin to rediscover a level of peace that we once enjoyed. With this being said, however, we need to take some time and get to the very heart of it all: living life with God. It may sound crazy, but while you may be able to play the game with others—even close friends—it's not so easy playing the game with God. You can try, but in the long run, you are only fooling yourself because God knows you better than anyone else. Or as my dad once told me, "Ron, the car looks great, but under the hood, it's still a mess."

Finding Peace from the Inside Out: Living Life with God

I think you would agree that we live in a world where life changes on a dime. Loss and the uncertainty that comes with it leave us unsettled, and it's hard to rise above it all and see the light. Sometimes it seems as if peace within our heart and soul is only wishful thinking. God, at times, seems distant and remote. It's hard to reconcile what we think we know about God with the way he works in this upside-down world. My episode of throwing rocks at God is only one story; there are many who find themselves in similar circumstances of wondering what to do, where to go, and asking why God doesn't seem to care when you need him the most. It can be confusing and overwhelming.

In the midst of confusion and uncertainty, however, there is a cosmic paradox of sorts just waiting to be found. As it turned out, God didn't reject my angry rocks or love me less because of them; he actually welcomed them and embraced them. He was well aware of my pain and frustration, and he didn't turn his back on me. He was simply listening *without judgment* as I poured out my heart and soul, and I'm not the first to realize this. The psalmists knew it some twenty-five hundred years ago.

The beauty of the Psalms is that they are raw. They are open-ended conversations with God that often describe the sentiments that we ourselves feel and carry inside. The psalmists were real people with real issues, real frustrations, and real disappointments. They used their writings to vent, to express anger, to rail at the same God we follow, and then they often sat back and waited for answers. In the midst of their strife, they often asked God to punish their enemies, they wondered why God would cause whatever it was they were going through, and they sometimes asked why some people have it so good when they have it so bad. It's a perplexing mystery, and yet at the same time, it's also a divine snapshot of living life with God. In many Psalms, by the time the ranting comes to a close, the writers would also express a level of resolute faith that is sometimes hard to reconcile. And herein rests the paradox, an odd and sometimes uncharacteristic combination of genuine frustration and unwavering faith; this is crazy. The young warrior David, who would someday become a king, is a great example of how frustration and faith can work hand in glove. He penned his thoughts as follows:

How much longer will you forget me, Lord? Forever? How much longer will you hide yourself from me? How long must I endure trouble? How long will sorrow fill my heart day and night? How long will my enemies triumph over me? Look at me, O Lord my God, and answer me. Restore my strength; don't let me die. Don't let my enemies say, "We have defeated him." Don't let them gloat over my downfall. I rely on your constant love; I will be glad, because you will rescue me. I will sing to you, O Lord, because you have been good to me.[43]

There are helpful encouragements that we can garner from a Psalm such as the one above. It's OK to ask hard questions of God. It's OK to let him know that what we're feeling sometimes goes deeper than our emotions and into the deepest recesses of our inner heart, and it's OK to cry out to him in the very midst of our raw anger and severe disappointment. The psalmists go on to reveal that God is always there to let us know that his love for us goes far beyond what we can understand. It is ever present, unyielding, complete, and flawless in every way. It never retreats. It surrounds us at all times. It never fades nor spoils. It is perfectly present at all times. We simply need to keep the eyes of our heart and soul open to it. It still puzzles me as to how all of this fits together. I find myself venturing back to the original meaning of Christmas, and it is here that the words of Matthew speak the loudest. In one simple word, he reminds us that we are never alone: *Immanuel*, which means, God with us.[44] Luke takes it a step further and reminds us that Immanuel came offering peace and favor to all humankind.[45] So as it turns out, in Christ, God is actually with us. We didn't invite him; he just showed up.

Then later in the book of Luke, when the religious leaders rejected a woman for simply washing the feet of Jesus, he (Immanuel) would say to her, *Go in peace; your faith has saved you.* And then again, at the end of his life, Immanuel would tell his closest followers, *Peace I leave with you; my peace I give to you.* The bottom line is that in Christ there is peace. We didn't ask for it. He just offers it. On the surface, however, the offer of peace can at times seem rather thin, sometimes irrelevant, and often quite evasive. In the turmoil of life, and all that it throws our way, the last thing we think of is the idea of peace. So what does *peace*, the kind that God offers, mean anyway?

> Peace (Greek, noun), a harmonized relationship between God and humankind, friendliness, a sense of rest and contentment resulting thereon. The corresponding Hebrew word, Shalom, primarily signifies wholeness. The Greek verb for peace denotes the idea of being reconciled, be it with God, or with one's friends or family members.[46]

In the New Testament, the word *peace* shows up in three very different shapes: peace *from* God, peace *with* God, and the peace *of* God, and each one has an incredibly rich and extremely helpful meaning.

> Grace, mercy and *peace from God* the Father and from Jesus Christ, the Father's Son, will be with us in truth and love.[47]

> Therefore, since we have been justified through faith, we have *peace with God* through our Lord Jesus Christ, through whom we have gained access by faith into this grace in which we now stand.[48]

> And the *peace of God*, which transcends all understanding, will guard your hearts and your minds in Christ Jesus.[49]

The *peace from God* means that God is the only genuine source of lasting peace; it is found in him and nowhere else. Here the word *from* is a preposition of source, basis, or origin. It is an unpredicted gift *offered* to everyone. This is *peace from God*. However *peace with God* means that God is the only one who can bring himself and humankind together. It is an unmerited reconciliatory gift *received*. Here the word *with* is a preposition of relationship. This is *peace with God*.

As most of you know, life can be very a rough ride, and it was the same with the followers of Jesus. Early on following him was thrilling and always an adventure. There was no telling what would come out of his mouth next, and he was always irritating someone. Then one day out of the blue, Jesus gathers his closest followers and shares that he was going to leave them, that they would in essence suffer loss, that all they've hoped for would vanish at his death, and that their dreams of what could be would be shattered in an instant. This is when Jesus tells them, "Peace I leave with you and peace I give to you."[50] A bit earlier, much to the dismay of the religious leaders, he would tell a woman, who out of a heart of profound love washed his feet with an expensive perfume, that because of her faith she could *go in peace.*[51] In both settings Jesus spoke of a different category of peace: the type of peace that Paul spoke of in Philippians 4:7 (above). Jesus speaks to it, and Paul defines it as the *peace of God.* Here the word *of* is a preposition of essence within. It's a *way of being* at our very core, and it is precisely why and how we can set the sum of our anxieties, our disappointments, our anger, our fears, and our sorrows directly upon the shoulders of the Crazy Shepherd. This is a deep-seated inward peace *granted.*

Life will most assuredly throw us a curveball, but if we can somehow muster the energy and courage to simply open our eyes, we will see the agent of true hope and peace: the Christ-child who ushers in unprecedented and unwavering peace in all its meanings. It is the peace *of* God that will carry us through the highest of the highs, through the lowest of the lows, and back toward the highest of highs again. This is the place where we live life with God in his perfect presence. It is a *peace from the inside out,* and while it's not always easy, it's worth every ounce of energy we can pour into it. But why does this level of peace within sometimes seem so elusive?

During one of our vacations at Virginia Beach, while Bonnie was still sleeping, I decided to go for a long run along on the boardwalk. It was windy, somewhat chilly, the waves were crashing in, and the rain had begun to fall. It was beautiful. What made it so beautiful was witnessing the incredible power of the ocean and the ability of the seagulls to not only navigate their way through the wind but also to find food in the midst of the storm. As the waves crashed in, I would run higher on the beach, and when the waves receded, I would run toward the water on the fresh wet sand. It was a blast. This went on for over an hour or so, and by the time I started my return, I was soaked, sandy, and dirty. While running back to the hotel, I laughed at my insanity, and when I looked up at the fourth floor of the hotel, I saw dozens of people running on treadmills in the fitness center. Safe. Dry. Listening to an iPod. Not talking to anyone. Running but not getting anywhere. They avoided getting wet, dirty, and windblown, but they also missed out on some of the greatest scenery on the planet. I couldn't wait to tell a few of my running friends; they would understand.

Like those runners on the fourth floor, some people do life in the same manner. They are just going through the motions, playing it safe, afraid of putting themselves out there, and not really going anywhere. I wonder if they will ever experience the thrill of doing life with God. They're either afraid, good at playing the game, or simply unwilling to go beyond their secret loneliness—that secret place inside where they can hide their deepest feelings and the brokenness that keeps them there. Something is holding them back. It's safe and comfortable. It's terrifying to think of doing anything else. Unfortunately the manifestations of playing the game, or living in one's secret loneliness, can be as harsh as addiction or depression, or as invisible as escapism while quietly keeping others at a safe distance. And what emerges is often an unwillingness to change. It is comfortable living there and easy to avoid the type of life change into which the Crazy Shepherd is calling us. True change often requires an uncomfortable paradigm shift, a rattling of our interpretive grid, one that if never stressed, pushed, or challenged keeps us where we are. I think people remain unchanged because they are unwilling to listen to the not-so-easy truth that God has to offer. This truth can create tension inside and can push us to think rather differently. These truths, if we let them, can redesign, reshape, and reform our beliefs, our attitudes, our behaviors, and our entire view of God and how he longs to restructure the entirety of who we are on the inside.

Oswald Chambers offers the following: "The greatest spiritual crisis comes when a person has to move a little farther on in his faith than the beliefs he has already accepted."[52] Sound familiar? Need a little help? Enter the Crazy Shepherd.

One day Jesus told Peter and all of his cohorts to climb inside a boat and go to the other side, then he left them on their own and journeyed off to pray by himself. As he was praying, those in the boat made their way across the lake and found themselves a considerable distance from the shore, and the winds began rock the boat quite severely. Sometime later Peter and the crew recognized Jesus as he was walking on the water toward them. Jesus, aware of their fear, assures them that there is no need to be afraid. Peter then, aware of the potential costs, asks Jesus to invite him to walk on the water, and of course, Jesus grants his request. Once out of the boat, however, after numerous successful steps, Peter loses his confidence and begins to sink. Jesus then rescues Peter.[53] I often wonder what Peter's friends might have thought as they watched him stepped out of the safety of the boat. Maybe they thought he was crazy. Anyone of them could have done so, but only Peter trusted and took a risk. Not the kind of trust that lacks evidence, but the kind of trust that weighs what we know and then takes the next step of resolute faith. After all if faith were something we simply embrace in the absence of risk or danger, as we rest comfortably in the boat, it wouldn't require trust. Peter, however, put his faith on the line and decided step out on trust.

On another occasion a rich young man asked Jesus what good thing he could do to obtain eternal life, and by the end of the conversation, Jesus ultimately told him to go sell everything he had and give it to the poor. This was something that the young man was not willing to do; the price was far too high.[54] If he did such a thing, his safety net would have been removed, and as such, it was too risky. The cost was too high. He had too much to lose. It's easy to have faith when all is well; it requires very little.

In these two stories, there is an obvious contrast in the choice that was made. Not an easy one, but one that was enormously difficult. Both Peter and the young man stood face-to-face with a difficult decision—to trust or not trust—and only one accepted the challenge that was wrought with risk and uncertainty. There are times in our lives we also must decide, and just as it was with Peter and the rich young man, it's rarely if ever easy. It's a difficult fact of life that regardless of the strength or the nature of our faith, or the depth of our relationship with God, or how much we pray, or how much we read the Bible, or how often we serve the poor and homeless, or go to church, we will experience loss, frustration, and severe disappointment, often to the point where we can't help but throw rocks. It's an unavoidable part of our existence, and it can push us to the limit. It is here, however, that we find ourselves at a crossroads. Will we allow our circumstances to define our faith, our life, and view of God, or will we trust the God who surrounds us with his unyielding love and ever-present peace? I know it sounds crazy, but there is an enormous difference between letting life define you and trusting God to the point where you let him help you define your circumstances.

(Journal entry, July 7, 2012 [edited for personal reasons])

Life in the Moment

Along the way of dealing with my grief, there have been many people telling me that they have been and will continue to pray for my heal-ing, and this was especially true when I embarked upon my one-month sabbatical. I'm truly overwhelmed by everyone's love and support. One of the first things I had to do, however, was try and figure out what healing looked like. It was an anomaly to me, and as such I needed some framework from which I could move forward. What is healing, and as the word itself implies, can you ever be healed?

In thinking through all of this, it slowly occurred to me that it depends a great deal upon where you are spiritually when you're hit with such devastation. (I'm sure that this is not new to most people.) What I mean by this is that in my grieving and navigating through the loss of Bonnie, I've never been angry or upset with God. Did her death conjure up numerous difficult questions? Sure, but in retrospect, he has been the life-giving eternal rock who has helped me hold it all together. The psalmists, who have walked more challenging paths than I, have mapped it out quite clearly. In other words, God has not been the area of my life that needs any sort of healing; I guess this was part of my confusion when people said they would pray for me to heal. While it has not always been the case, the vertical side of my life was at this time not a part for concern. So, I had to then look at the relational and emotional side of life, if you will, the horizontal dimension. This is the foremost area of my healing struggle.

The idea of being healed in the depth of my emotions, or in the extent of my relationships, is right now too much to ask. I'm quite convinced that healing is never actually complete; there is no such thing as being healed. In this arena of life then, grief is incurable. There is a vast difference between incurable and terminal, at least in my mind. Terminal means that whatever you're dealing with will be the cause of your death; it's like those who are suffering from terminal cancer. As heartbreaking as it is, it's the cancer that will at some point end their life. Incurable, on the other hand, means that what you're dealing with will not end your life, it will simply affect it over the course of your life; it never really goes away. In other words, it's never healed.

It has only been one year [since Bonnie's death], but in my mind right now, the type of grief that is brought on by such a devastating and heartbreaking loss is incurable; it never truly goes away; it's ever present. So rather than healing, I'm learning to cope with my incurable grief. Ironically it was much the same as Bonnie, in that she had to learn to cope with her incurable systemic lupus, and cope she did. Once again, while neither of us knew it, during the thirty-seven years of our marriage, she was teaching me how to cope with the incurable. The grand challenge for her, however, was that her disease was both incurable and terminal, and we were both well aware of how it may unfold. So we chose to live it out the best we could and make the best of a life-changing situation. Side by side we traveled to places many don't get to see, at times had more than enough, and other times never knew how we would get by. We supported each other at every major crossroads in the good times and the bad, dove headfirst into vocational ministry, enjoyed five-star resorts, and served the poor together in the Dominican Republic, Mexico, and Detroit. And even in the midst of her ever-present, ongoing pain, we truly enjoyed the fullness of the life that God gave us.

As it turned out, she unknowingly prepared me to deal with that which is incurable: a broken heart and fractured soul. She will always be here to remind me that life is far too short to dwell on what can't be done, but to live fully in the moment of his unwarranted grace, the unprecedented peace, and the matchless love of the God who now watches her fly on the wings of eagles, run and never grow weary, and dance with the Jesus she loved more than anything or anyone else. So I guess not being healed really doesn't matter all that much; my incurable grief helps me remember who she was and how she shaped my life. Like she taught me, it's how we move forward with our incurable grief that makes all the difference in this crazy life and in the lives of those around us, and it is here that I can now begin to move forward and rediscover the nature of a raw hope, and once again dream larger-than-life dreams in the midst of my incurable broken heart. I'm beginning to slowly move beyond my secret loneliness; she was crazy before I knew what crazy was.

This is only one small example of living life with God and discovering peace inside that works its way out in life. God doesn't mind our rocks. He embraces them, and better yet, in the middle of it all, he embraces us every day, every hour, every minute, every moment in time. He is always here just waiting to be found, and we need look no further than in the present. I hope my personal stories help you in some small way because the extremely difficult turns in life are far from easy. They are grueling at times. But in the midst of it all, let's not overlook the relentless and unyielding love of God, who we are in him, and how we can still somehow love others as ourselves. Our experiences, whether good or bad, play a profoundly formative role in the development of an empathetic heart and soul. I know, it isn't fair, and you may not be there yet, but this I also know, there are others just like us who need to be loved in the same way we love to be loved.

Living life with God, a trusted friend, as we hold so very close the extraordinary peace he offers, as difficult as it may seem at times, is one very real answer to moving beyond our secret loneliness. In the next chapter, we change gears and begin looking at the specific trademarks of those who are crazy enough to step out of the boat and into the sometimes-dangerous water of following the Crazy Shepherd.

Crazy Peace, in all its forms, is the way of crazy sheep, and it's yours for the asking.

CHAPTER 6 CRAZY LIFE | *Moving into the Dangerous Footsteps of Jesus*

Warning: this chapter and the next is where crazy gets totally off-road crazy.

It was a Friday evening, and as we sat there and ate dinner, all I could think of was what was next on my schedule. It had been an exasperating week and the weekend didn't look much brighter. Sensing a need for some immediate personal relief, and before thinking about it, I heard the following command pass through my lips: "As soon as we're done with dinner, we're going to see *Robin Hood*, starring Russell Crowe!" It was a slow motion, out-of-body experience as I sat there in silence just waiting for the push back. However, without blinking an eye, and unmoved by my emphatic tone, my wife simply looked over her glasses and reminded me that earlier in the week we had already decided to go, and once again suggested I see a psychiatrist as soon as possible. So we quietly finished dinner and then went to see the movie. I loved every minute of it. She tolerated it.

Some time later a friend of mine would suggest that I most likely had a man crush; Russell Crowe was my hero. *Robin Hood, Master and Commander, 3:10 to Yuma, Proof of Life, Cinderella Man*, and *Gladiator*; I've seen them all at least three times, some even more, and they never grow old. They spark something deep inside. While I'm not convinced about the man crush, maybe there is a reason that I'm drawn to the larger-than-life characters he regularly portrays. Glorious adventure, thrill, risk, danger, rescue, romance, superheroes and supervillains; there is a reason movie theaters are packed each and every day. Much like me, maybe people are looking for something deeper. But at the same time, maybe we also have become grotesquely satisfied with the vicarious approach to life. It costs us nothing except the price of a ticket and a bag of popcorn. At the end of the day, however, it's only a momentary prescription to a desire deep within, so we sit back and wait for the next movie staring Russell Crowe.

Maybe we've collectively made the decision to play it safe, and as such, we often find ourselves going through the motions. We get up early, grab a cup of coffee as we're running out the door, go to work, come home, take the kids to soccer, come back home, have dinner, watch some TV, go to bed, and repeat the cycle. Then on weekends we go see a movie. Don't get me wrong, these are all important and sometimes essential activities, but in the midst of it all, maybe there is something deeper that we're desperately missing. Have we inadvertently fallen victim to an unfortunate myth that playing it safe, comfortable, and predictable is the best approach to life? You can see it in the way some people live their lives, organize their time, and raise their kids. For example, the other day I saw a seven-year-old boy riding his bike on a paved biking path near my house. He was wearing a helmet, kneepads, elbow pads, and riding gloves, and as he rode along the path, his parents kept chirping at him, *Be careful. Don't fall. Go slow, and stay on the paved path.* But when you looked at this kid's face, you could almost see the flames of adventure shooting out his eyes; he so wanted to ride in the dirt and ride fast. My heart sank because they didn't seem to get it. It seems to me that without personally experiencing the thrill of the dirt and the dangers that come with it, the odds of this kid spending most of his time playing *Mortal Combat* on his computer safe in his bedroom seem somewhat high. I get the helmet—I wear one on every ride—but ditch the pads, and let this little boy ride in the dirt. And when he falls down and scrapes his knee, wipe it off, tell him his is doing great, and then encourage him to get back out there and go faster. It's who he is. It's how he is wired.

Some churches are no different. We're told to be nice, don't cause trouble, don't rock the boat, stay between the lines, follow the rules, getting hurt is not worth the risk, don't push back, don't ask tough questions, don't challenge leadership, don't reveal what's going on inside your gut, don't offend anyone, play it safe, and by all means, stay on the paved path of religious predictability. I remember sitting in the front row one Sunday when a pastor invited the high school kids to go on a local mission trip. He was passionate in his presentation and genuine in his request, but he also knew that most parents of this suburban area would be fearful of their kids going to the inner city. So he promised that if they let their kids go on the trip, they would be safe, and God would most assuredly protect them. I remember thinking, *How can you say that? How can you make such a promise?* The last I checked, Jesus never promised safety; safety is a myth.

We, the human race, wherever we live, whatever language we speak, and whatever situation we find ourselves in, are hand-wired by the living God for adventure, risk, danger, rescue, expedition, romance, quest, and pursuit. It's who we are at our very core, and to suggest or even promise a life of predictable safety is tantamount to nonsense. Or is it just me?

Jesus Was No Mr. Rogers

One of my favorite experiences is what scuba divers call neutral buoyancy. So one afternoon as we were diving near a huge reef, my dive buddy and I decided to venture off the reef so we could hover in a few hundred feet of water. Once we could no longer see the reef or the bottom, we dropped down to fifty feet and stabilized ourselves using our buoyancy compensators. Neutral buoyancy allows you to stay at your desired depth and then using your breathing you can control your ascent and descent. Breath in, and you slowly ascend. Exhale, and you slowly descend. The best part, however, is when you hold your breath at midpoint and simply hover; it's as if there is no gravity. Then you close your eyes, and before long you can't tell if you're upside down or right side up. Self-induced vertigo, spatial disorientation, and not knowing you're upside down is so much fun. Sometimes.

During the first century, the religious leaders managed to find themselves in a state of self-induced vertigo, and they needed a swift kick in the pants. These religious leaders, although early on well intended, had managed to create a religious system where those who subscribed to certain behaviors, which were defined by them, were rewarded, and those who didn't were out of favor, ostracized, and rejected. One's religious value was often determined by one's social status, heritage, physical appearance, gender, or ethnicity. It got so bad that they actually believed that God rejoiced at the death of a sinner (*sinner* referring to someone with no religious, spiritual, social, moral, or cultural value. Again, as defined by them). The problem is that they were upside-down and didn't know it. They had no clue that spiritual and religious vertigo had set in, so guess who shows up? Jesus, the crazy one.

Imagine yourself as a religious leader. It's not really that difficult because, while we may not admit it, most people think they can do a better job than those who are leading today. So give it try. Pretend you're leading a religious movement, and everything seems to be going rather well. Attendance is good, and the money is rolling in. People finally seem to have their act together, and the troublemakers are no longer an issue. While inside the building with your religious friends, you're rather comfortable and no longer confronted with the rabble of society: those who don't look like you, live like you, view marriage and sexuality like you, talk like you, vote like you, believe like you, smell like you, or spend like you. They are out, and you are in. Life is good and safe. Imagining this is not so much of a stretch, is it?

One day, however, a new religious leader shows up, and he is different, very different. He's so different that he gets upset with you, the religious leader, and begins to call you names. He refers to you and others like you as a bunch of snakes, a brood of vipers, blind fools, wicked hypocrites, and whitewashed tombs (clean in the outside and yet dead on the inside). He offends you, hurts your feelings, and challenges your logic and cultural sensibilities. He speaks the truth with authority, calls it like it is, offers no apology, and in a very short period of time, he manages to push you and your friends to the point where you want him dead, and the sooner the better. This is precisely what happened when the Crazy Shepherd arrived on the scene.

It makes me chuckle because I can almost hear his mom saying to him, "Jesus, be nice. Don't offend anyone, don't hurt anyone's feelings, don't push back, don't ask hard questions, don't cause trouble, don't scrape your knee, play it safe, and stay on the paved path." But as you may know, he refused to do so. There was far too much at stake, and by the religious and cultural standards of the first century, he took the essence of authentic religion and pushed it to the extreme. Jesus had the audacity to lecture that it's not only right to forgive your friends but also your worst enemies, which was a sign of failure and defeat in the first century. He taught that true leaders are those who lead with humility, selflessly putting others ahead of themselves. This was a sign of weakness in the first century. Jesus taught that real freedom is found in becoming a slave, nothing more than property to be owned. He taught that infants and children are precious gifts to be honored and cared for—a total reversal of the view of human life in the first century. He washed the feet of a traitor—an unheard-of submissive act that ran against the grain of being a king in the first century. He cast out demons—actions of someone who was controlled by the devil in the first century. He claimed to be God—an outlandish, blasphemous act deserving death in the first century. He refused to worship Caesar—an act of treason in the first century. He touched lepers, healed the blind, restored the paralyzed, hung out with a prostitute, ate with tax cheats, and sat down at a well for a long conversation with the lowest of lows: a Samaritan woman who had five husbands. All of the aforementioned encounters were considered despicable, unclean, and defiling events for someone who referred to himself as the Son of God. Let there be no doubt; Jesus was no Mr. Rogers, and he would have nothing to do with drifting hopelessly in the upside-down ocean of the status quo.

Jesus was the antitheses of safe. He was dangerous, and in the eyes of some, he was an outlaw. He was called a drunkard, out of his mind, crazy beyond hope, and yet, in the eyes of many others, those on the outside looking in, he was a precursor to Robin Hood, if you will. He didn't want to turn the world upside down; he wanted to turn it *right side up*. The world, both religiously and culturally, was already upside down, and worse yet, clueless. Sometimes I wonder if we are experiencing a form of self-induced spiritual vertigo. Are we living our Christian life on the safe path of predictability, playing the Christian game, and simply going through the motions? Do the exceedingly hard teachings of Jesus offend us to the point where we quietly dismiss them as irrelevant or even old-fashioned? Do we systematically place the demands of his life and teaching on the shelf so we can live in the center of what we presume to be acceptable and relevant? If so, the question then becomes, how can we begin to move from the safe and easy life into the dangerous footsteps of Jesus? This assumes, of course, that you want to figure it all out, and that living on the other side of safe is something you want earnestly to explore. If so, please read on.

The journey toward some answers begins with a story and a deeper issue at hand. Over the years I've had the privilege of working with a handful of young men and women who have felt the nudge to enter into vocational ministry. At some point somewhere in life they have felt called by God to become a church leader, a pastor, or missionary. I'm always moved when they ask for help and counsel. There is no doubt in my mind that I've made numerous mistakes in helping them realize what God has in store for them as they explore the nature and depth of their calling. It's the imperfect leading the imperfect. On one occasion, as I was meeting with a couple who I had been working with for some time, they shared their decision that it was time to leave the calling that we all thought was so strong. After some discussion they simply and very politely moved on. As far as I know, they are still living in the peace and safety of life as is, and my fear of all fears is that they will never see or experience the dangerous side of life as leaders of a movement that is far from easy and safe. It's difficult thinking that you may have played a part in stepping on someone's dreams, but after many hours alone on the trails, it came to my attention that if their calling and passion is genuine, God won't leave them alone until they decide to get on with it and step back into the danger of living life without the safety net. I hope they do—they have much to offer, and so do you.

There is a difference between the gladiator and the spectator. Only the gladiator knows what it's like on the coliseum floor. There it is either life or death, and while the thought of fighting to the death may sound like an over-statement, it's very true. Our time on this earth is a battle between life and death. Maybe not in the physical realm, but most certainly in the spiritual realm, and there is nothing more grievous than to be physically alive but spiri-tually dead. Playing it safe is wrought with apathy and indifference. It does nothing to right the injustices of this world. It's a losing proposition that leaves people in the dust of hopelessness and despair. It does nothing to the situation we find ourselves in, a world where people are hungry and desperate for something much deeper and everlasting. If we're not willing to break free from the safety myth and enter into the dangerous coliseum, then who will? Who will stand up and fight for the invisible and those who have no voice? Who will take a stand against the failure of educating our inner-city children? Who will say no to the ugly grip of self-centeredness and greed? Who will step in and help break the chains of generational poverty? Who will make room in their calendar so they can deliver the much-needed meals to the sick and lonely senior citizens in your neighborhood? Who will develop the next micro business nonprofit that can help people escape the grip of finan-cial hardship? Who will muster up the courage to help stop sex trafficking in your area? (Think this isn't an issue in your community? Think again). Who will reach out and help families with children who have special needs in your community? Who will cut the lawn of your neighbor who is being cared for by in-home hospice? This list is endless, so suffice it to say, who will hand out that next cold cup of water and, with it, that simple prayer?

If not you, then who? Maybe it's time that we simply decide to get off the paved path of predictable safety and step onto the crazy dirt road of becoming marvelously dangerous.

Becoming Dangerous

OK, back to Robin Hood (and Russell Crowe, of course). Robin Hood lived on the edge of danger, but he was only dangerous to certain people. Robin and his band of thieves were only a threat to those who wanted power and control at the cost of those who simply wanted freedom. There is a familiar ring of truth here, in that our battle is much the same and yet very much different. So before we can move forward to what it means to become dangerous, we must be very certain of where the real battle and subsequent dangers rest.

Over the past twenty years, it has been my experience that for some the battle and the dangers therein find their way between those who follow Jesus and those who don't. Their anger then is directed at those who don't share their Christian family values, political views, or established doctrinal beliefs, and once again this approach often cultivates an *us vs. them* conflict. Whether it's Christian vs. non-Christian or church vs. church, it can get out of control. Maybe you have seen it. Maybe you've experienced it. Maybe you are part of it. But the fact that it exists begs the question, to whom are crazy sheep actually becoming dangerous? Is their so-called enemy those with whom they work, go to school, or go the movies together? Is their real battle with those who don't share their views on this or that? Does it have to be us vs. anyone else? It is here that the apostle Paul reminds us of the true nature of the larger conflict at hand.

A final word: Be strong in the Lord and in his mighty power. Put on all of God's armor so that you will be able to stand firm against all strategies of the devil. For we are not fighting against flesh-and-blood enemies, but against evil rulers and authorities of the unseen world, against mighty powers in this dark world, and against evil spirits in the heavenly places.[55]

As you can see, the real conflict, struggle, or battle is not against other people, whoever they may be, but against the principalities of darkness, the forces of evil in this world. To put it another way, when crazy sheep begin to rise above apathy, indifference, greed, self-absorption, egocentrism, ethnocentrism, consumerism, selfishness, and how greatness is defined, they become dangerous only to the forces of evil. Their real enemies are not those for whom Jesus willingly surrendered his life and died a humiliating death on a cross between two thieves. The Crazy Shepherd sacrificed his life for anyone and everyone, and then without hesitation, asked his crazy sheep to do the same. Yes, this sounds absurd if not insane because the life he calls his sheep into is a life wrought with danger. There can be great risk in standing up for the endemic rights of others, speaking out against injustices that have become intrinsic, speaking up on behalf of the voiceless, or demanding systemic change that requires a cosmic shift in how things are presently done. This may sound counterintuitive, but to make a lasting impact in this profoundly hurting world, being a crazy sheep in the eyes of the forces that want to keep you on the safe path of harmless predictability is absolutely necessary.

What Is It That Makes His Sheep Crazy?

Before we actually look at a few examples of what crazy sheep look like, we need to examine what makes them crazy to begin with. In other words, what are some of the qualities of crazy sheep? To this I offer the following: crazy sheep willingly obey the Good Shepherd and will follow him anywhere regardless of the personal cost. Why? Because they know that much more is at stake than the comfort of the sheep pen. They understand that there are many more lost sheep than there are found ones, and following him will cost them something. Crazy sheep will follow the Good Shepherd to places unknown and aren't afraid to climb mountains that they've never seen before, mountains that seem insurmountable. Why? They know that the pure thrill of it all is found in the climb with the Good Shepherd, not the summit. How so?

- It's during the climb that they find out who they really are deep down inside. Normal sheep play the game; crazy ones climb deep inside.

- It's during the climb that they find out what they're willing to endure for the mission of the Good Shepherd. Normal sheep think of themselves; crazy ones put others first.

- It's during the climb that character is built and humility begins to set in. Normal sheep rarely change; crazy ones let Jesus change, mold, and shape their very core.

- It's during the climb for their life that they learn the depth of unequivocally trusting the Good Shepherd. Normal sheep shrink back; crazy ones attach themselves to Christ and let him pull them up the mountain.

This too is counterintuitive in that the summit isn't the goal. The goal is knowing that during the climb, you have fought the good fight, you have run the good race with all that you have, you have done your best to climb the insurmountable mountain before you, and along the way, you have trusted the Good Shepherd. To this crazy approach to life, Oswald Chambers offers the following insight:

> If I can stay calm, faithful, and unconfused while in the middle of the turmoil of life, the goal of the purpose of God is being accomplished in me. God is not working toward a particular finish—His purpose is the process itself.[56]

Maybe it is time for you to take a dangerous step out of the coliseum seat and onto the coliseum floor. If so, what does following in the dangerous footsteps of the Crazy Shepherd actually look like? In my first book, *The Religion of Jesus*, I talked about how Jesus rescues us from (*out of*) one thing and at the same time rescues us *into* something else.[57] It is *into the something else* that places his crazy sheep directly on the path of becoming dangerous, and what follows are two examples of the *into something else*: greatness and contentment, two key building blocks of the crazy life.

The Crazy Metrics of Greatness

We live in a world where greatness is often defined using terms like *winners* and *losers*. Awards, championships, accolades, titles, achievement, wealth, or one's educational accomplishments are often held high as the true measures of greatness. Great leaders are those who give great speeches. Great companies are those that make the most profit. Great people are those who have the most influence. Greatness is making is it big in Hollywood or Wall Street. I live in a world where greatness is occasionally measured as big. Big church, big budget, big numbers, big production, big stage, big billboards, big crosses, big name, big book deals. Please don't misunderstand; crazy sheep follow a big God, and there's nothing inherently wrong with big when it comes out of a humble heart. It is here that big can become an aftereffect, or an outcome, of something even much bigger: a sold out, Jesus-centered servant's heart that humbly embraces the crazy life and all that it entails.[58] Big, however, does not necessarily denote greatness. Pastor John Ortberg wrote the following about the meaning of greatness:

> [In the Roman world,] the way of the hero exalted many wonderful qualities: courage and excellence and persistence, overcoming obstacles, self-discipline, and self-mastery. But humility was not an admired quality. It was not considered desirable. What was desirable was greatness. Historian

Robin Lane Fox wrote, "Among pagan authors, humility had almost never been a term of commendation. It belonged with ignoble and abject characters…The humble belonged with the abject, the mean, the unworthy." But another way was emerging. A poor rabbi, who never wrote "The Deeds of the Divine Carpenter," said to his friends, "You know that the rulers in this world lord it over their people, and officials flaunt their authority over those under them." No Roman would have been offended by this observation of Jesus. The whole point of making it to the top of the pecking order is you get to peck. But what Jesus said next would offend: "Not so with you. Instead, whoever wants to become great among you must be your servant." [59]

As we've discussed, the metrics of greatness that were once embraced in the Roman world are often used today. Not much has really changed; it just wears a different set of clothes. If we look at greatness through the lens of the Crazy Shepherd, however, we come up with a very different picture of greatness. When you look at how he lived, read what he taught, and examine what he celebrated, you begin to see a new metric of greatness. For example, when you evaluate his life:

- What was the measure of Christ's greatness? *Becoming a self-less servant.*

- (By human measurements) what did he accomplish? *He irritated most everyone and managed to get executed.*

- What did his organization look like when he died? *Unorganized chaos.*

- How big was his original organization? *Twelve.*

- How did they respond to his suffering? *Abandonment.*

- Who was part of his organization? *Losers, outcasts, rejects, tax collectors, and sinners.*

- How many books did he write? *Zero.*

- What would his movement become? *The largest movement in human history.*

To this new metric of greatness, there is an episode in the life and teachings of Jesus that truly stands out. Jesus had just completed another in-depth explanation regarding the nature of his mission and purpose for heading toward Jerusalem. Jesus had mapped out his plan on a few other occasions, but this one took place only days before he was to enter the city for the final time. As they were about to enter Jerusalem, Jesus sat his disciples down and again described his purpose rather clearly. Leaving no room for misunderstanding, he told them the following:

> Again he took the Twelve aside and told them what was going to happen to him. "We are going up to Jerusalem," he said, "and the Son of Man will be delivered over to the chief priests and the teachers of the law. They will condemn him to death and will hand him over to the Gentiles, who will mock him and spit on him, flog him and kill him. Three days later he will rise."[60]

It seems clear enough. The King of kings, the one who claimed to be God, the highly anticipated Messiah, the Anointed One, the Son of David, the Son of Man, the one who could have called upon legions of angels to spare him pain and suffering, was about to submit himself to the governing and religious authorities. Furthermore, once in Jerusalem, he was going to willingly subject himself to an obscenely humiliating death. As was mentioned earlier, it was death on a cross between two obscure criminals. Now one would think that his *chosen twelve* would have been moved to tears or captivated by his incredible sacrifice and willingness to personally model the new era of greatness, a life of sacrificial humble service to others, whoever they may be.

But what happens next invites us into the mind and thinking of the first century of which his twelve closest followers were not immune. No sooner than Jesus's words passed his lips, two of his treasured disciples asked him the following:

Then James and John, the sons of Zebedee, came to him. "Teacher," they said, "we want you to do for us whatever we ask." "What do you want me to do for you?" he asked. They replied, "Let one of us sit at your right and the other at your left in your glory."[61]

You read this correctly. In the midst of his servant's life and selfless actions, Jesus's closest followers wanted positions of greatness, and greatness to them meant more authority and power. In a commentary regarding this totally absurd and out-of-place request, Walter Wessel notes the following:

> The request made by James and John seems utterly preposterous. They wanted Jesus to do for them whatever they asked, a carte blanche request! When Jesus asked what that might be, their answer was that they might have the positions of highest honor in the messianic kingdom. They wanted a place of [supreme] prominence and recognition [not the true measure of greatness of which Jesus was about to demonstrate].[62]

But unraveled by the question, as was quoted earlier, Jesus's answer puts the measure of true greatness into perspective, a timeless and much needed lesson for all of us.

> Jesus called them together and said, "You know that those who are regarded as rulers of the Gentiles lord it over them, and their high officials exercise authority over them. Not so with you. Instead, whoever wants to become great among you must be your servant, and whoever wants to be first must be slave of all. For even the Son of Man did not come to be served, but to serve, and to give his life as a ransom for many."[63]

As it turned out, it wouldn't be until after his resurrection that his disciples would truly begin to understand and enter into this new metric of greatness. But this is OK; the Crazy Shepherd is patient with his crazy sheep. This young rabbi was redefining greatness not only in his teaching but also in the totality of his behavior.

Another example of this new metric of greatness is found in one of the least talked about apostles: Andrew, the brother of the apostle Peter, fully devoted himself to the Crazy Shepherd. If you are at all familiar with the New Testament Gospel accounts as it relates to the actions of the apostles and how the church expanded in the book of Acts, then you are aware that Andrew's brother was typically center stage. Peter garnered all attention, while Andrew, on the other hand, was backstage. And even today when Christian speakers talk of leadership, they often refer to Peter and the lessons we can learn from him. They rarely, if ever, speak of Andrew, and maybe Andrew would have preferred it this way. He was an inconspicuous servant who paid attention to insignificant details. To the role of Andrew, John MacArthur comments, "He is more of a silhouette than a portrait in Scriptures."[64]

What most don't know about Andrew is that, according to tradition, he was martyred for his faith. Like Jesus, his death was also on a cross. He was crucified near Athens in southern Greece. He reportedly introduced the wife of the Roman governor to Christ, but that governor then demanded she recant her new confession. When she refused, it was then that Andrew was executed, and while hanging on the cross, he continued to speak of the one true Jesus who can rescue the lost and restore the found.[65] We don't hear much about Andrew, but it seems as if greatness is often found in those who live behind the scenes, in those who live an inconspicuous life of willing, humble service to those who live on the other side of the good life. No fanfare. No spotlights. No book deals. There is just the heart and actions of a humble, selfless sheep. This is crazy greatness, and maybe this is what Jesus meant when he said, "Be especially careful when you are trying to be good so that you don't make a performance out of it. It might be good theater, but the God who made you won't be applauding"[66].

The Crazy Life of Contentment

He who dies with the most toys wins! This was the motto of the five of us: my four brothers and me. Growing up in the 1970s and 1980s, we all had managed to work our way to reasonably successful careers. For the most part, life was good, and as we all know, success often means more income, and more income usually means more toys. So the race had begun. It was loads of fun, and we really didn't take the race all that seriously. It was simply a time in our lives where we were all doing rather well and just wanted to celebrate our success with each other. None of us got really carried away. Later in life, however, my wife and I chose to take a different path, a path that led us into stepping away from my business career and into a life vocational ministry. At every crossroad to get where we wanted to go in our new endeavor, we were supported and encouraged by my all of my brothers. I am forever grateful for how they embraced our decision to go off-road, and it was during this experience that Bonnie and I, like may others, had to learn what contentment was all about.

Before he found himself face-to-face with Jesus while traveling to the city of Damascus, the apostle Paul was a person high of esteem, highly educated, and was considered an exceptional religious leader. He wanted for nothing. Once Paul yielded his life to the Crazy Shepherd, however, everything changed. In short, he stepped onto the coliseum floor and thus set aside the good life for the crazy life, and in doing so, he often found himself in need. It is here, in the center of need, that Paul defines the nature of crazy contentment. In a letter to Christ followers in the city of Philippi, as he was expressing his deep gratitude for their ongoing support, he maps it out this way:

> I am not saying this because I am in need, for I have learned to be content whatever the circumstances. I know what it is to be in need, and I know what it is to have plenty. I have learned the secret of being content in any and every situation, whether well fed or hungry, whether living in plenty or in want. I can do all this through him who gives me strength.[67]

A bit later Timothy, one of Paul's students, does the same. In speaking to the often-found tension between relentlessly pursuing financial gain and a life of persistently following in the footsteps of the Crazy Shepherd, he explains the nature of contentment as follows: "Godliness with contentment is great gain. For we brought nothing into the world, and we can take nothing out of it."[68]

Theologian Homer A. Kent, Jr., explains that finding one's *contentment* in Christ would have been viewed as unique, if not off-road crazy:

> In Stoic philosophy, content described the person who accepted impassively whatever came. Circumstances that he could not change were regarded as the will of God, and fretting was useless. This philosophy fostered a self-sufficiency in which all the resources needed for life were within him or herself.[69]

Contentment is best defined as *sufficiency*. And when we place it in the context of what Paul and Timothy were talking about, it describes the totality of their satisfaction and completeness in Christ. Sufficiency in Christ, however, ran against the grain of first-century thinking; this is why it was, and can be today, considered crazy. This is a difficult concept to grasp. It can be confusing because what does one's sufficiency in Christ have to do with being content with one's circumstance, whatever it may be? Everything.

There are many ways this component of the crazy life can unfold. Some choose to set aside a career and enter into vocational ministry, and others choose to simply live on less so they can give more to the cause of the Crazy Shepherd. In either scenario, the adjustment and subsequent search for contentment is intentional. There are other times, however, when the same search is forced by economic hard times. It's no secret that the material things of life come and go, here today and gone tomorrow. Given the economic crash of 2008 and 2009, it doesn't take much of an imagination to realize this is so very true. Life changes on a dime. It's out of our control, and all that we once had can be gone in an instant. What happens when all those things that brought us satisfaction disappear? If having much brings contentment, what happens when much is gone? In times like these, what will often surface is our deep-seated need for Christ and those he has placed in our lives. The point I'm trying to make is this: when life is centered on the Crazy Shepherd, and those who love us as we love to be loved, we can experience contentment in any situation we may find ourselves in at any given moment.

As I reflect back on my thirty-seven years with Bonnie, twenty-one of which were in vocational ministry, we wanted for nothing really. We would frequently look back and wonder how we did it or how we managed to get through the month. Honestly we accredited it all to the Crazy Shepherd and the incredible people he brought our way. Contentment was no elusive dream; it became real. It sounds so crazy, but having less, be it intentional or otherwise, was actually having more.[70] To be sure, godliness with contentment is great gain, but it is here that crazy contentment takes an unexpected crazy twist.

Being content in one's circumstance is not absence of zeal, passion, focus, risk, vision, and the off-road life that Jesus offers. Get this: even in our times of need, we always managed to go on a short-term mission trip to be of assistance to those in deeper need. Bonnie always found a way for me to go wherever, whenever God nudged. In other words contentment does not necessarily mean being satisfied with the way things are. Nor does it mean that we don't work hard so we can provide for our family. At one point the two of us worked five jobs. Contentment simply means finding the sum of our sufficiency, our satisfaction, and our adequacy in Christ. But here's the oxymoronic twist: it is very much possible to be content and discontent at the same time. In other words one can be content in one's own circumstance and yet at the same time be discontent with the condition others find themselves in: living in poverty, homelessness, loneliness, hunger, or being lost in wealth and success. Ironically if you do indeed find your sufficiency in Christ, he often will breathe into your heart and soul a level of discontent that will get you out of the seats and onto the coliseum floor. In your mind you begin to see no other viable option because you slowly start spending less and less time worrying about yourself. You become an advocate for those who deeply need that which they may never see on their own, and before you know it, you become a selfless, crazy sheep. Whether you believe it or not, it happens quite regularly.

Meet Michael and Caryn Young. While attending a Hope for Orphans seminar conducted by Family Life Ministries in the fall of 2009, Caryn was unaware of the path that God was initiating. Under the belief that she was attending an information-gathering meeting, and the prospect of possibly starting an orphan ministry for her church, a new sense of unsettledness was birthed in Caryn's heart that would not become clear for over two years. In the midst of her contentment, God seemed to have different plans for both her and her husband Mike.

Since becoming followers of the Crazy Shepherd, Mike and Caryn were engaged in a wide variety of serving ministries in various churches in various locations, but there was one geographical area that captivated both of their hearts. They had a desire to serve in the city of Detroit. By January of 2011, Caryn had discovered a hovel of a building near the midtown area that had the potential of becoming a safe haven for low-income housing. The thought was to create a faith-based housing cooperative for people in need and to work in conjunction with an existing and successful Detroit ministry. Having worked in the city for years, Caryn and Mike had developed a comfort level with real-estate transactions, and converting this ramshackle apartment should not be a problem. However, due to a variety of legal and financial obstacles, the plan failed to materialize. Undaunted by the setback, Caryn continued to explore potential locations, and by August she had discovered a larger apartment building closer to midtown. It was perfect in that it was in much better condition and far more suitable, but in the weeks to come, they would discover that building lacked ample parking. Much to their dismay, the building's parking lot had already been sold. Another setback. However, as Caryn continued to pray for answers, she received an e-mail regarding a possible meeting with Faith Communities Coalition on Foster Care.[71] The gathering was designed to discuss the challenges faced by teens in the foster care system. At this meeting Caryn discovered that there existed a significant demand for affordable housing for teens that were aging out of the Michigan foster care system, and this would ultimately become the expression of an idea that began to slowly break its way to the surface in the fall of 2009. So on February 8, 2012, the Central Detroit Community of Hope was born.

During the ensuing months, many volunteers, the dream-makers, gathered around Mike and Caryn and began to renovate and paint their newly acquired house (which is a God-story in and of itself). With the help of many, this building became much more than a house. It became a safe home dedicated to providing a Christ-centered living environment for young women aging out of the foster care program. As crazy at it may seem, the Crazy Shepherd had taken Mike and Caryn to precisely where he wanted them. Contentment does not mean being satisfied with the life as is.[72]

The metrics of greatness and living in the tension between contentment and discontent are only two examples of the life the crazy life. Stories like Mike and Caryn's continue to emerge. One theologian calls this phenomenon *cascading grace*, and it describes those moments in time when crazy sheep take steps that are often viewed as insignificant, but in the grand scheme of life, they are monumental. One small step leads to another and then another, and before you know it, you are standing in the middle of your dream to help others who simply need a concrete glimpse of tangible hope. Let there be no doubt; you can be perfectly content and wildly discontent at the same time.

This is the crazy life of crazy sheep as they simply follow in the footsteps of the Crazy Shepherd. Want to jump in? If so, then all you need to do is look around in your own community. Read the newspaper. Talk to your neighbors. Strike up a conversation with a dreamer. Talk with your school district leaders or your fire department. Pay close attention and take a walk in your city or village. Because unlike what you may have heard, these opportunities don't come knocking on your door. You have to seek them out, and as you're looking around, if you ask the Crazy Shepherd to strike a chord of discontent in your heart and soul, at some point, he will. But then be willing to put whatever necessary into tangible action with a few other crazies like you. And before you know it, you'll find yourself on the coliseum floor. Welcome. There is plenty of room, but as you already know, it's not going to be easy.

Crazy sheep, living the crazy life, as they faithfully walk in the dangerous footsteps of the Crazy Shepherd, are everywhere. Are you ready? Excellent! However, before you run out the door, you may want to read the next chapter. Why? Being a crazy sheep requires an atypical and sometimes misunderstood mindset. I call it *life in the center of regardless.*

CHAPTER 7   A CRAZY FINAL THOUGHT | *Moving into the Center of Regardless*

Not that long ago, I was having a conversation with a friend when he said to me, "God has blessed me with good health, a great job, and three great kids." I politely agreed, but as I was driving back home, it got me to asking, Why does it seem as if God blesses some, and yet others are apparently not so blessed? In other words why do some people have more blessings than others? It can be very confusing, and not knowing why can create an atmosphere of feeling less-than because God is apparently blessing only certain people. So we ask, what am I doing wrong? What's wrong with me? Why does it appear as if God shows some level of favoritism? But on the other hand, do blessings really hinge on certain behaviors or practices? Do they depend upon one's obedience or one's measure of faith? Are blessings a reward for this or that? Or is the absence of them some sort of punishment? So many questions but few answers.

I don't pretend to understand life and all it brings our way. There is so much beyond my ability to understand in the short time we're on this earth. It's sometimes hard to make sense out of the senseless and find peace in the midst of the chaos and noise. When asked why, we often feel compelled to explain the actions or inactions of God. We sometimes mistakenly (in my mind) assume that he is directly responsible for anything and everything that takes place, and as I mentioned earlier, we often discount the actions and motives of the evil one who longs to steal and destroy our dreams and aspirations. We live in a broken and upside-down world, and we sometimes wonder where God is in all of this. All too often we live our Christian life with slogans and bumper stickers that help us cope with the unknown or explain life in a manner that comforts us. We feel safe in knowing and vulnerable when we have no answers.

We've talked about this incident before, but on one occasion early in the ministry life of Jesus, he was speaking to a very large crowd on the side of a mountain who gathered to hear the words of this new rabbi. Unlike the other teachers of the law, he was one who taught with great power and surprising authority, but he also spoke about the arrival of a new Kingdom. It was the nature of this new Kingdom that captured everyone's attention. To some it was good news, and yet to the aforementioned religious leaders, the news was not so good. The not-so-good-news crowd was afraid of losing influence, power, and control, for they had managed to construct a system by which they determined the value of people, especially the value of those who were sitting on the mountainside. The good-news crowd was sitting on said mountainside, and much to the dissatisfaction of the not-so-good-news people, they began to hear how they were actually the ones who were blessed, according to the metrics of this newly arrived Kingdom.

To the other rabbis, the good-news crowd was nothing more than the dregs of society, the losers and the misfits, the social outcasts and sinners of no particular consequence or concern. This new rabbi's message, however, was one that would change everything, and it went something like this:

One day as he saw the crowds gathering, Jesus went up on the mountainside and sat down. His disciples gathered around him, and he began to teach them.

"God blesses those who are poor and realize their need for him, for the Kingdom of Heaven is theirs.

God blesses those who mourn, for they will be comforted.

God blesses those who are humble, for they will inherit the whole earth.

God blesses those who hunger and thirst for justice, for they will be satisfied.

God blesses those who are merciful, for they will be shown mercy.

God blesses those whose hearts are pure, for they will see God.

God blesses those who work for peace, for they will be called the children of God.

God blesses those who are persecuted for doing right, for the Kingdom of Heaven is theirs."[73]

What made the not-so-good-news teachers so angry was the very idea that God blesses those who they considered outside the scope of God's blessing. In their mind, blessing, or being esteemed and highly valued by God, was based on personal performance, one's social status, material possessions, family heritage, physical appearance, good health, and how they conducted themselves. To hear that those gathered on the mountainside were the ones who were actually blessed, highly esteemed, and honored by God was a grotesquely foreign idea. It ran in total opposition to the views of the other rabbis, and it would be the spark that set in motion the plans to execute this new teacher.

It wasn't that long ago when I was having coffee with a young lady who was a Christ follower and genuinely frustrated. She was at a point in her life where it wasn't going that well and in her mind it wasn't going to get better any time soon. As we talked it became apparent that she was convinced that the more you do for God, the more you get blessed by him, and conversely, if God's not blessing you, then you must be doing something wrong. She was trying to figure out what she was doing wrong that caused God to no longer bless her. After our third cup of coffee, I finally asked her, "If our behavior is what determines blessing, then why does it seem like good things happen to bad people and bad things happen to good people? We see it all the time. How do you explain it?" After some further

Crazy Shepherd ~ Crazy Sheep

discussion, we agreed that good things do happen to some very bad people and concluded that there must be more to blessings from God than what we see on the surface, and maybe the Crazy Shepherd has something to say about it.

This outlaw rabbi taught that, in his Kingdom, blessings are so much deeper and far more sustainable than what we may or may not be going through at any given time in this life. Blessings aren't based upon certain behaviors or the metrics of a cast culture that measures the value of life in terms of ones performance, lot in life, socio-economics, educational status, ethnicity, or religious heritage. Blessings indeed transcend circumstance.

The Crazy Center of Regardless

There is a story in the Old Testament about three young Jewish men who found themselves in the classic dilemma. The word *dilemma* quite literally means (a choice) between two lemons. You might say they found themselves between the proverbial rock and a hard place, and it is here that one's choices, either way, seems to have difficult and often dangerous consequences. Their names were Shadrach, Meshach, and Abednego, and it is in their story that we begin to see how placing God at the center of life can influence the decisions that we make, in spite of the potential outcome.

One day the King of Babylon, Nebuchadnezzar, had his minions construct a very large and rather impressive gold statue in honor of himself. Kings in those days were considered deity, and as such, he commanded everyone in his Kingdom, at the sound of the music, to fall on their knees and worship the statue, him. If you wanted to live, you worshipped the king, and if you refused, there was only one other option: death by furnace. It was really that simple. By this time the three young men, Shadrach, Meshach, and Abednego had managed to find their way into positions of influence as spiritual advisors to the king. But this appointment by the king didn't sit well with the king's other spiritual advisors; they wanted the three young men to go away, so death by furnace seemed like a solution. So the next time the music started, they closely observed the young Jewish advisors and discovered that they quietly refused to worship the king's image, which meant they refused to worship the king. Perfect! They quickly and rather joyfully reported this blatant act of disobedience to the king, who then summoned the young men to inquire whether or not the accusation was true. Herein rests the dilemma. To say yes meant death by furnace, and to say no meant a denial of the one true God in whom they believed and trusted. So the king, in an unprecedented act of compassion, granted them one more opportunity to bow in worship, but again they refused to worship him. The king was furious and posed a question: "You are going to be thrown in the blazing furnace, and what god can rescue you from my hand?"

It is in the answer of these three young men that we discover what it means to be crazy by entering into the *center of regardless*. To the king they simply replied, "The God we serve is able to deliver us from your hand, O king. But even if he does not, we want you to know that we will not serve your gods nor worship the golden image of yourself that you set up."[74] *Regardless* of God's action or inaction, they refused to cave in to the pressure. The choice to disobey the king was the choice that led to death, and the choice to cave was the choice that led to life. But these three young men knew something much larger was at stake. The majority of us rarely if ever find ourselves in this position, that is, taking a stand that means literal life or death. However this isn't the only point of the story. What these three young men were saying, albeit indirectly, is that in this life they wouldn't allow the so-called blessings of this physical life to add to or take away from what they knew as central, which is the deep measure of love, the unwavering grace, the unwarranted mercy, and the ability of the living God to rescue them whenever and from if he so chooses. They didn't need to ask why or why not. They quietly and obediently stood their ground in the center of *regardless*.

The faith of crazy sheep gets tested almost every day in small and large ways. And all of the spiritual practices, be they praying, fasting, tithing, solitude, worship, serving, memorization, or study, to name a few, won't deliver us from the hard side of life. That's not why we engage in them. Because we live in a broken and sometimes painful world where bad things happen, no one is immune from them, and God is not necessarily executing his punishment or deliverance just because we did or didn't do something.

Have you ever found yourself at a place in life when everything seems to be spinning out of control? I vividly recall one week in particular when I was getting ready for a three-week vacation, preparing the message for the coming Sunday, working on two projects at home, visiting a few people in the hospital, getting the car ready for the trip, talking with those who would cover for me while gone, and at the same time I was trying to help my wife with her own preparations. It was a grand balancing act, and it was all that I could do to keep it all together. I have no doubt that you can relate. It might look something like this

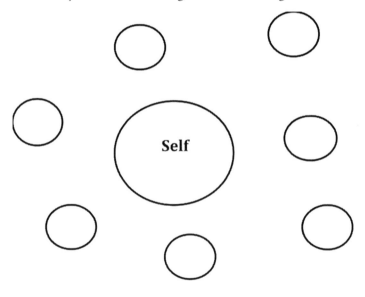

Fig. I

This is how most of us live each and every day, trying to balance it all. Most of us live in a world of circles that represent a certain dynamic or aspect of life. Job, spouse, kids, parents, family, church, PTO, soccer, dance classes, vacation, grandparents, friends, neighbors, God, and whatever else you want to throw in the mix. They are all circles that we're trying to balance, and we're at the center of these circles. They all revolve around *self*, and we go through life doing our best to maintain a sense of balance and stability. Sound familiar? The fact of the matter, however, is that we will never balance them all. Just about the time we think it's all under control, an event takes place that causes us to lose equilibrium, and we subsequently drop a ball or two. It's unavoidable. It's not possible to balance all that life throws our way. Have you ever been there? Are you there now? If so, take heart, because just as it was with playing it safe, *the balanced life is a myth*. There is, however, a better way to live in this upside down, busy world. It is through the Crazy Shepherd. As Jesus was preparing his closest followers for his departure, he was mapping out what it would take for them to move forward with his mission once he was gone. While they didn't fully realize it at the time, he was building into them an alternative to the so-called balanced life. In one of his last in-depth conversations with his disciples, he made the following shocking statement:

> Remain in me, as I also remain in you. No branch can bear fruit by itself; it must remain in the vine. Neither can you bear fruit unless you remain in me. "I am the vine; you are the branches. If you remain in me and I in you, you will bear much fruit; apart from me you can do nothing."[75]

As you can see, the Crazy Shepherd explains that his sheep must remain *in* him if they are to begin producing the *fruits* of life, fruits that are a natural by-product of an intimate relationship with the Vine-grower. This fruit is joy, peace, patience, kindness, and faithfulness, just to name a few.[76] But just as it was for his early followers, this unusual approach to life has to be learned. It doesn't come natural when we're trying to balance everything life throws our way. There is, as Jesus taught his disciples, an alternative to consider.

When describing the nature of the identity of Christ-followers, the New Testament writers repeatedly use the prepositional phrase *in Christ.*[77] Thus crazy sheep are *in* the Crazy Shepherd. The preposition *in* is a word of relational position. It's a word of identity that reflects the idea of centeredness, Christ at the center of life. It might look like this

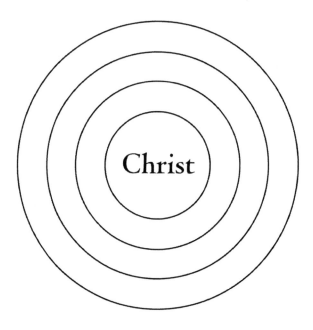

Fig. 2

Christ at the center means being located in the middle of, not on the cusp of. Christ, not in one of the circles that surrounds our life, but Christ at the very center of them. Everything else in our life revolves around him, and this is precisely what makes the crazy life in this upside-down world possible.

There is a fundamental life-changing difference between keeping Christ on the edge of our life and placing him in the very center of it. Whenever I perform a wedding, I marvel at the idea of how two people who at one time never heard of each other can over time grow so incredibly close that they are almost inseparable. In many ways it's a divine mystery. Over time you can somehow tell when a marriage is doing well. A person who once lived on the periphery now lives in the center of the other; it's as if they begin to see what the other sees and hear what the other hears. I've been there. It can happen. If it's true in marriage, how much more is it true with Christ? You can comfortably leave him in the periphery of your life, or you can place him in the very center of it. As with marriage, it too can be a grandiose over-the-top love affair. His best interests become your best interests, what he sees you begin to see, and what brings him to tears will do the same in you. Christ at the center of regardless affects the choices you make, how you raise your kids, how you treat your spouse, how you spend your time, and, yes, how you spend your money. Our deepest joy and fulfillment in this crazy life is found *in* the Crazy Shepherd. Peace and contentment are not contingent upon circumstances. In Christ, we are able to rise above whatever life throws our way. After all, Jesus himself said, "Seek first his kingdom and righteousness, and these things will be given to you as well."[78] It sounds so very crazy, but Christ in the center affects everything, *everything*. If you can name it, Christ at the center of regardless changes it.

Blessing and Gratitude

On my way to meet a friend, I got to thinking. Maybe there is a subtle and yet important distinction between blessings and gratitude. Maybe blessings, being highly esteemed by God, transcend what takes place on this earth. Maybe the quintessential meaning of God's blessings are found in the very nature of the intimate relationship we have with him *regardless* of what life is like in the here and now. Maybe blessings are also discovered in the nature of the relationships we have with others who walk the same path. Maybe blessings are profoundly everlasting and radically independent of time and circumstance.

Gratitude, however, is both different and yet much the same as blessings. Gratitude is different in that it is more of a response than it is something received; it comes from a place deep within the heart and soul. Gratitude seeks no resolution. It finds its way through the unanswered questions and the mystery therein. As it is with blessings, gratitude also transcends one's place in life. Gratitude is an expression of pure thanksgiving, knowing that we did nothing to either deserve or not deserve what we may or may not be experiencing. Blessings can be discovered most anywhere and everywhere; they are there for those who look for them. On the issue of blessings and gratitude, a dear friend wrote me the following:

We don't love God for the gifts he gives but because he is God, the lover of our souls. We trust him as good and loving, so we walk, in faith, in the path he has shown us. Then there's always the (church) body issue. We aren't given everything we each desperately need individually, and so in the (church) body we find others who share and build us up; they complete the unity we long for. Don't think of community so much in terms of "getting stuff done" using our gifts but in terms of community making whole our need for relationship. What is truly something is the way we live our lives in gratitude, peace, contentment, trust, and in faith. Those are the (crazy) heroes of faith. Those are the people I want to emulate.

So as it turns out, I can now begin to see that blessings aren't limited to what I have or don't have, or what I once had and now can't have. Maybe they do indeed come in many shapes and sizes, go beyond the here and now, and the *why* behind them all is really not that important. Knowing *why* doesn't really change anything. Furthermore, maybe in my quest for why, I've missed that which is standing right in front of me: the Crazy Shepherd and the crazy sheep who will follow him anywhere. Because it seems as if crazy sheep go out of their way to help those who can't see so well, and in doing so, they begin to see life and the blessings therein a bit clearer themselves as they too live in the *center of regardless.*

As difficult as this may seem, this is where true life, a deeply transformed life, begins, by placing the Author of it at the very center of it, *in the center of regardless.* Are you ready to live here, in the center of regardless? I hope you take some time and invite Him in. Take a long walk in the woods, go sit on the beach, or find a quiet place somewhere. Take whatever time you need to prayerfully ask the Crazy Shepherd to occupy center stage in your life. If you sincerely ask him, he will do it. This is my deepest prayer and wish for you and the primary reason I wrote this crazy book.

After all, much like their Crazy Shepherd, crazy sheep:

- *Live on both sides of crazy love.* Why? Because when he looks into your eyes, you take his breath away, and then turning to the heavens, he confidently proclaims, "See everyone, I told you so, no worminess here. What's not to love?" Crazy love and crazy forgiveness is the way of crazy sheep.

- *Live on both sides of crazy hope.* Why? Because in all of its depth and richness, you too can offer that cold cup of water and a simple prayer. There is a hope worth embracing and a hope worth extending to others. Crazy hope: two sides of the same coin. It's the way of crazy sheep.

- *Live on both sides of their crazy dreams.* Why? Because along the path of never giving up, new dreams may emerge, ones that you never saw coming or thought you would ever have. As it turns out, the Crazy Shepherd is always up to something. Crazy dreams. It's the way of crazy sheep.

- *Live on all sides of crazy peace.* Why? Because as difficult as it may seem, at times we hold so very close the extraordinary peace that he offers:

peace with God. Crazy peace. It's most assuredly the way of crazy sheep.

- *Walk dangerously in the crazy footsteps of Jesus.* Why? Because before you know it, you'll realize that you're no longer a spectator, and as you look around, you'll discover that you're in good company. Crazy sheep, faithfully, humbly, and obediently walking in the dangerous footsteps of the Crazy Shepherd, are everywhere.

- *Find life in the center of regardless.* Why? Because this is precisely where the truly transformed life begins, by placing the Author of life at the very center of it, *regardless.*

Thanks for reading one man's story of hope that was found in the Crazy Good Shepherd. I hope it helped you see yourself and your life differently as you too follow him.

Crazy Shepherd, Crazy Sheep
It Really Is This Simple

Epilogue

The irony of getting from here to there

The Unavoidable Crazy Shepherd

As I mentioned in the introduction, crazy sheep hang on every word, every promise, every thought, every dream, and every command of the crazy and ever-present Good Shepherd. One of the grand challenges, however, is working through and learning to embrace the entirety of his teachings. It's a lifelong endeavor, and along the way, it's easy to view them as a sort of theological buffet where you can pick and choose what fits your tastes and appetite at any given time, but this was never his intent. This is especially true with his teaching regarding his own identity, but why do I bring this up now? I hear this with some degree of regularity: *I love Jesus and want to live like him. He was a great teacher and a fine role model. No doubt, if we all lived as he lived, this world would be a better place. But I don't adhere to the claims that he was God. This seems like a stretch to me.* So what's the answer? How do we try and live as Jesus lived and yet come to terms with who he said he was? Furthermore, how do we connect the dots between how he lived and what he accomplished on the Cross?

Like it or not, the vast majority of what we know about Jesus comes from the first four books of the New Testament, the Gospels. In these four books, the authors describe both Jesus's incredible life and his audacious claims regarding his own identity. As first-hand witnesses to his life, his mission, his purpose, and his identity, these writers also shared statements such as, "Look, the Lamb of God who takes away the sin of the world."[79] Moreover, as their stories unfold, they also share his teachings as to how his crazy sheep should live. So this is precisely why we begin our quest for craziness in these four books. They are the sum of his teachings, his life, and his assertions as to who he is, why he came, and what he did. This being said, common sense would dictate that it's not logical to walk in his footsteps without coming to terms with his self-proclaimed identity and ultimate rescue mission. If it were logical, however, you wouldn't be considered crazy. Putting it another way, why would you want to follow the teachings of someone who claims to be God but isn't? Why would you even consider following someone who claimed his willing and successful sacrifice for your wrongdoings but then didn't follow through with this claim? Finally if his claims related to his identity are in-deed misguided, how can we trust anything else he said or did? These are the questions we must navigate through, but here's what brings us back to where we started.

Accepting his teaching and yet questioning his claims to be God are the very reasons Jesus was called crazy by the religious leaders when he first arrived on the scene. They thought he was out of his mind. But if you stop and think about it, either way he is crazy. He is either out of his mind (crazy) and not worth following, or he is crazy to the point where he is the only one who can offer both love and hope that we all truly desire and need. He is either a crazy misguided teacher who shares a few good ideas of how we can live, or he is the one and only Good Shepherd who was crazy enough to offer his life for the ransom of all. The character and nature of his love was then, and still is, per-fect in every way. His grace-laced sacrificial life was crazy long before we knew what crazy was, and it is here that we must make a decision. It's between you and him. You have to decide this on your own. Which crazy do you want to follow: a crazy, misguided teacher or the one and only Crazy Good Shepherd? At the end of the day, it's this simple. Well?

If you've come this far and want to step into the mix, here are a few simple suggestions that will help get you started. To climb inside the sometimes-dangerous footsteps of the Crazy Shepherd, there are two things to consider. One is far from new, and the other we haven't talked about before.

1. Jump onboard the Jesus train.

The coliseum floor is only an invite away. This is how it all starts—by stepping up to the platform, welcoming Jesus into your life, and getting on the train. In some circles this is called an invitation; in other places this is called surrendering to Christ. Then there are those like me who say that this an extremely personal decision to entrust one's entire life to the Crazy Shepherd by an act of trust (aka. faith) and then following in his footsteps to the best of one's ability. Call it what you like, but the end result is the same: you become one of his sheep well on your way to becoming crazy. Because, whether you like it or not, much like my Patton Street Gang friends, you are now guilty by association.

I hope this book has helped you catch a glimpse of how this way of life is actually the most rewarding and fulfilling way to live, in the center of regardless. There are alternatives, but in the grand exploration of life, they are dead ends. They lead to nowhere in particular and will leave you in the dust of uncertainty, confusion, chaos, and disappointment. Walking the path of a crazy sheep, however, will get you where you need to be, walking in the very footsteps of the One who became like us that we might become like him. It cost him everything. It was his gift to us, and he is waiting for you to simply embrace it and get on board. It's up to you. You have a decision to make.

Once on the train, however, start looking for a God-movement in your community, a church that stirs your heart and soul, one that is soundly centered on the person and teachings of the Crazy Shepherd. You can't separate them. Look for a church that is not afraid or offended at your questions, and make sure they are sold out to addressing the holistic needs of others. You know, that cold cup of water and a simple prayer that comes with it. The various chapters and topics in this book may help you find that place you can call home. It won't be the perfect church. They don't exist, but being part of one is a central teaching of the Crazy Shepherd, so never stop looking. However, once you find one jump on board with both feet. Talk to someone in leadership and get involved. Think long term. Look for a place to serve, and if it's not starting something new, be a crazy dream-maker. Remember, crazy dreamers need you.

2. Focus your Bible-reading on the Gospels, and along the way, let them read you.
The Gospels are nothing more and nothing less than stories of Jesus, who he was, what he did, who he claimed to be, and how he lived. So as you read them, please take your time, pray before you start, and let them sink in. As you read them, know that something, be it ever so small, is going to take place: *transformation.* The fine art of transformation (learning to live like Jesus) is like peeling an onion, layer after layer needs to get peeled away. These layers are our intellect and the will; layers of not-yet-seen virtue, character, ethics, and morality; and moreover, the layers of our heart and soul, all of which can be very fragile. Again, Oswald Chambers once wrote, "The greatest spiritual crisis comes when a person has to move a little farther on in his faith than the beliefs he has already accepted."[80] This is transformation.

The most challenging layer, however, is the layer of our perception. For example, last year I was having a cup of coffee with a friend when he said he was outside the scope of God's love. His actions over time led him to believe that God no longer loved him, cared about him, or even knew he existed. This was his perception, and as we all know, perception is reality. So, there he sat, head in hand. Our layers of what we perceive to be real, however, are not always true, and sometimes we need to let God intercede and peel these layers of perception away. Here is how it typically unfolds:

- The deeper we dig into God's story, *the deeper he digs into ours.*

- The deeper God digs into our story, *the more we see others and ourselves differently.*

- The more we see others and ourselves differently, *the further we are able to go.*

- The further we are able to go, *the deeper we dig into God's story.*

Like Shrek explains to Donkey, we are very much like onions. And peeling away layer after layer of perception, fear, and uncertainty is the process of living it out, and as God peels each layer away, we slowly learn to walk in the footsteps of the Crazy Shepherd. The Book that's not really about you was actually written for you. So place yourself in their shoes, in their stories, and along the way, ask yourself, what would Jesus say to me? For example, take the story of the woman who was brought before Jesus with shame written all over her face to the point that she could only stare at the ground. What did Jesus say to her?[81] What was her reality? How did Jesus speak to her reality? Is this your reality? How did Jesus treat and interact with this woman? Did he reject, condemn, or ridicule her? Was she really outside the scope of God's love? No. And neither are you. Let this truth become your new reality as well.

This is the fine art, and lifelong cycle, of learning, living, and walking in the risky and often uncertain footsteps of Jesus, and one day we will look back astonished and marvel at what God has done both in us and through us. It's a sight to behold. So maybe it's time for you to get on with it and make your way to the coliseum floor. After all, spectators are a dime a dozen.

The real adventure comes when you are willing to get in on the action. If I can do it, so can you. I know you can.

Acknowledgments (My Dream-Makers)

Those Who Make It All Possible

Like I mentioned in *The Religion of Jesus*, engaging in any meaningful endeavor requires a network of people who make it all possible. C. S. Lewis defined friends as those who know the dreams of your heart and then regularly speak those dreams back to you. To this truth I would simply add that friends also help turn our dreams into reality.

My dream-makers are:

- Dr. Larry Sherman. He always encouraged me to pursue my larger-than-life dreams. I'll always remember him, my coach.
- Ken. Your constant, atypical theological questions push me off the fence, but this is what brothers are for. Your encouragement is life-giving.
- Don and Martha. I have no words. Your friendship is priceless.
- Drew and Amy. You help make it possible to do what I do, and as soon as I figure it out, I'll let you know.
- Val, Rob, and Sandy. Thanks for proofreading my various dribbles early on in this quest.
- Amy, Pam, Julie, and Jessi. Thanks for reading what I thought was the final draft and answering my silly questions.

It is truly God's gift to have people in your life who believe in you when you don't believe in yourself, encourage you when you're so very discouraged, and love you when you are hard to love. Yes, Martha, I've finally realized that I'm a blessed man.

About the Author

Ronald Gelaude is a retired church-planting pastor with the Great Lakes Conference of the Evangelical Covenant Church and lives in Pinckney, Michigan. Ronald is a graduate of William Tyndale College (BRE, pastoral studies, 1994), Michigan Theological Seminary (master of theological studies, 1997), and Eastern Michigan University (master of communication studies, 2001). Ronald was married to Bonnie Gelaude for thirty-seven years. She passed on July 7, 2011. Ron continues to pursue God's call to serve the local church wherever it may take him.

ENDNOTES

Preface

[1] Benjamin Franklin, *The Autobiography of Benjamin Franklin*, notes by Charles W. Elliot, LLD (public domain), page 18.

Introduction

[2] John 10:19.

[3] John 10:14-16.

[4] Mark 3:20-21.

[5] John 10:9-10, The Message.

[6] John 6:60.

Chapter I

[7] Mark 12:29-31

[8] Using Christ's answer to the lawyer's question as the only command that needs to be followed presents some challenges in that there are many other commands given by him as to how his followers are to live. Exploring them, however, is beyond the scope of this book.

[9] An excellent reference for these Greek words is *Vine's Expository Dictionary of New Testament Words*, ed. W. E. Vine, Merrill F. Unger, William White, Jr. (Nashville, TN: Thomas Nelson, 1985).

[10]   2 Corinthians 5:14; Ephesians 2:4; 3:19. Found in *Vine's Expository Dictionary of New Testament Words*, ed. W. E. Vine, Merrill F. Unger, William White, Jr. (Nashville, TN: Thomas Nelson, 1985), page 382.

[11]   Inspired by Timothy Keller, *The Freedom of Self-Forgetfulness: The Path to the True Christian Joy* (Farington, UK: 10Publishing, 2012).

[12]   John 13:1-5, New Living Translation.

[13]   Taken from *The Expositor's Bible Commentary*, vol. 9 (Zondervan, 1984), page 90. Used by permission of Zondervan.

[14]   Paraphrase of John 8:2-11.

[15]   *The International Standard Bible Encyclopedia*, ed, James Orr. OSNOVA Publications (Hendrickson Publishers,1994), Kindle location: 14610-14618. Example: Luke 6:36.

[16]   John 1:10-12, New Living Translation (emphasis mine).

[17]   Romans 8:35, 38-39, New Living Translation.

Chapter 2

[18]   Matthew 22:15-22 (emphasis mine).

[19]   Matthew 5:43-47, New Living Translation (emphasis mine).

[20]   Matthew 18:21, New Living Translation.

[21]   *The Expositor's Bible Commentary*, vol. 8. (Zondervan, 1984), page 405. Used by permission of Zondervan.

[22]   The situation may remain unsafe even if the person is remorseful; it's OK to keep safe boundaries in tact.

Chapter 3

[23]   Franklin, *The Autobiography of Benjamin Franklin.*

[24]   Proverbs 13:12.

[25]   *The International Standard Bible Encyclopedia*, Kindle location: 175851-175862.

[26]   John 14:1-3.

[27]   John 10:10, Good News Translation (emphasis mine).

[28]   Mark 1:39-42, New Living Translation (emphasis mine).

[29]   Matthew 25:31-40.

[30]   Proverbs 31:8-9.

[31]   I Peter 3:15.

Chapter 4

[32]   Jake Gyllenhaal, Chris Cooper, and Laura Dern, *October Sky*, produced by Charles Gordon and Larry J. Franco, directed by Joe Johnson (Universal Pictures,1999). Based on *Rocket Boys* by Homer Hickam.

[33]   The term *religious others* refers to those who hold to an extremely strict view of religion and would cringe at the thought of my recommending a movie instead of reading the Bible. Taken from *The Religion of Jesus* by Ron Gelaude. Copyright Ronald C. Gelaude, 2012. All rights reserved. Available at www.createspace.com/3783407.

[34]   Acts 4:13.

[35]   N. T. Wright, *Simply Jesus: A New Vision of Who He Was, What He Did, and Why He Matters* (New York: HarperOne, 2011), page 217.

[36] John Ortberg, *Jesus: Who Is This Man? The Unpredictable Impact of the Inescapable Jesus* (Grand Rapids: Zondervan, 2012), page 187-188. Used by permission of Zondervan.

[37] Luke 5:1-11, New Living Translation.

[38] Wright, *Simply Jesus,* page 219.

[39] Matthew 28:18-20, New Living Translation.

[40] A combination of Psalm 34:18-19 and Matthew 11:28-29.

Chapter 5

[41] While she never went on another international mission trip, she would go with me to New Orleans to help the victims of hurricane Katrina. My incredible wife would hobble along as she carried moldy rubbish to the curb, and then she would often pray with the ladies who had just lost everything. It was a sight to behold.

[42] Proverbs 27:6, 9; 16:24.

[43] Psalm 13, Good News Translation.

[44] Matthew 1:23.

[45] Luke 2:14.

[46] Vine et al., *Vine's Expository Dictionary of New Testament Words,* page 464. Used by permission.

[47] 2 John 1:3 (emphasis mine).

[48] Romans 5:1-2 (emphasis mine).

[49] Philippians 4:7 (emphasis mine).

[50] John 14:27.

[51] Luke 7:50.

[52]   Oswald Chambers, *My Utmost for His Highest*, ed. James Reimann (Grand Rapids: Discovery House, 1992). Used by permission of Discovery House Publishers, September 15th.

[53]   Matthew 14:22-33.

[54]   Matthew 19:16-22.

Chapter 6

[55]   Ephesians 6:10-12, New Living Translation.

[56]   Chambers, *My Utmost for His Highest*, July 28th.

[57]   Ron Gelaude, *The Religion of Jesus*. Copyright Ron Gelaude, 2012. All rights reserved. Available at www.createspace.com/3783407.

[58]   There are many churches like this, and one such church is LifeChurch. tv. All of the incredible resources they offer are free of charge. They ask for nothing in return. This too is crazy greatness.

[59]   Ortberg, *Jesus: Who Is This Man?*, page 79.

[60]   Mark 10:32-34.

[61]   Mark 10: 35-37.

[62]   *The Expositor's Bible Commentary*, vol. 8, pages 719-729, (comments in brackets mine).

[63]   Mark 10:42-45.

[64]   John MacArthur, *Twelve Ordinary Men: How the Master Shaped His Disciples for Greatness, and What He Wants to Do with You* (Nashville, TN: Thomas Nelson, 2002), page 74. Used by permission.

[65]   It was in *Twelve Ordinary Men* that I learned of Andrew's life.

[66]   Matthew 6:1, The Message.

67   Philippians 4:11-13.

68   I Timothy 6:6-7.

69   *The Expositor's Bible Commentary*, vol. 11, page 154.

70   It is extremely important to note that there are those who have incredible skills, work ethic, talents, and gifts that position them to earn large sums of money, and as such, they live on the wealthy end of the spectrum. My personal experience is that those who do find themselves in this situation often live extremely generous lives as well, but more often than not, their generosity is behind the scenes, without spotlight, or fanfare. Wealth can be an incredible blessing when combined with the right heart.

71   Faith Communities Coalition on Foster Care (faithcommunitiescoalition. org).

72   You can read much more about Michael and Caryn's incredible story on their website (centraldetroitcommunityofhope.org), and if you are able, please donate to their cause.

Chapter 7

73   Matthew 5:1-10, New Living Translation.

74   An interpretive paraphrase of Daniel 2:1-18.

75   John 15:4-5.

76   Galatians 5:22-23.

77   Romans 8:1; I Corinthians 1:30; Ephesians 3:12 (just to name a few).

78   Matthew 6:33.

Epilogue

[79]   John 1:29, a statement by John "the Baptist" as he saw Jesus coming toward him.

[80]   Chambers, *My Utmost for His Highest*, September 15th.

[81]   John 8:2-11.

Made in the USA
San Bernardino, CA
29 April 2015